Editor
Torrey K. Maloof

Editor in Chief
Karen J. Goldfluss, M.S. Ed.

Creative Director
Sarah M. Fournier

Cover Artist
Sarah Kim

Illustrator
Mark Mason

Art Coordinator
Renée Mc Elwee

Imaging
Amanda R. Harter

Publisher
Mary D. Smith, M.S. Ed.

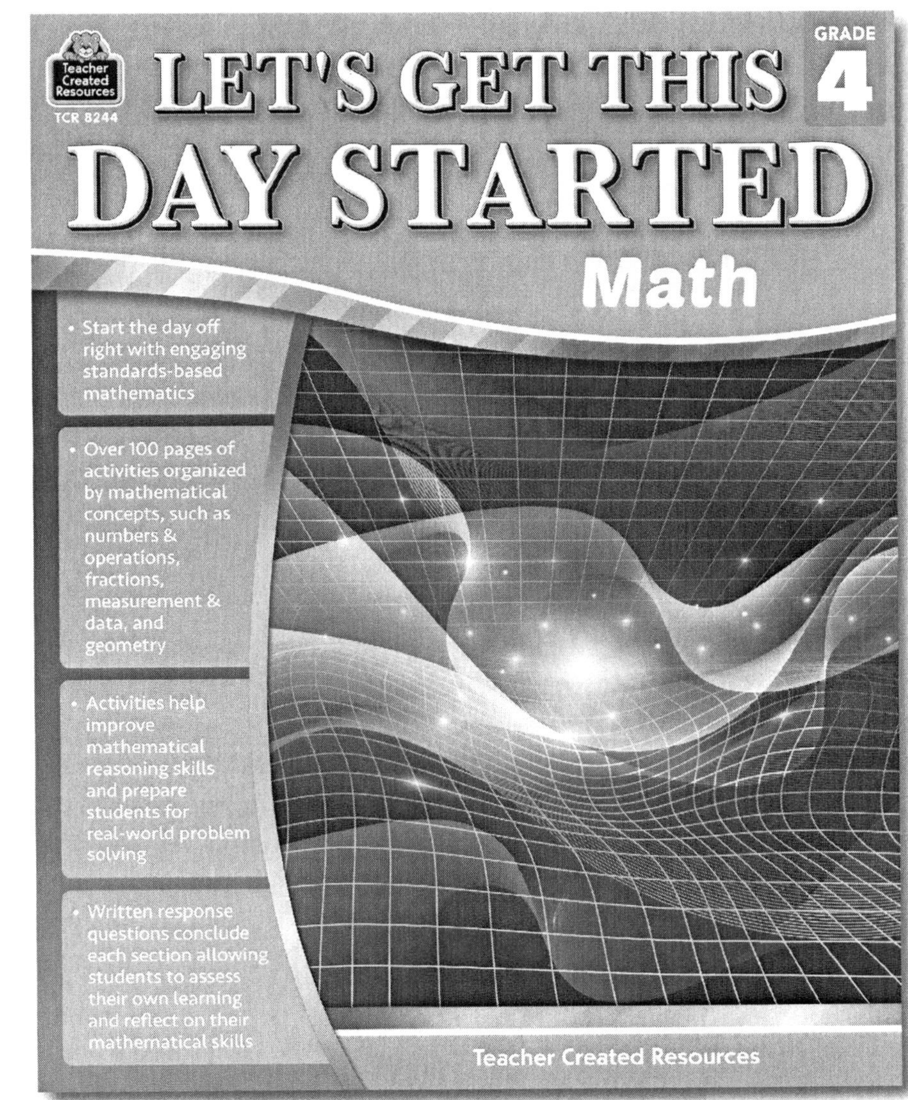
Teacher Created Resources
TCR 8244
LET'S GET THIS DAY STARTED
GRADE 4
Math
• Start the day off right with engaging standards-based mathematics
• Over 100 pages of activities organized by mathematical concepts, such as numbers & operations, fractions, measurement & data, and geometry
• Activities help improve mathematical reasoning skills and prepare students for real-world problem solving
• Written response questions conclude each section allowing students to assess their own learning and reflect on their mathematical skills
Teacher Created Resources

Author
Kristy Stark

D1604804

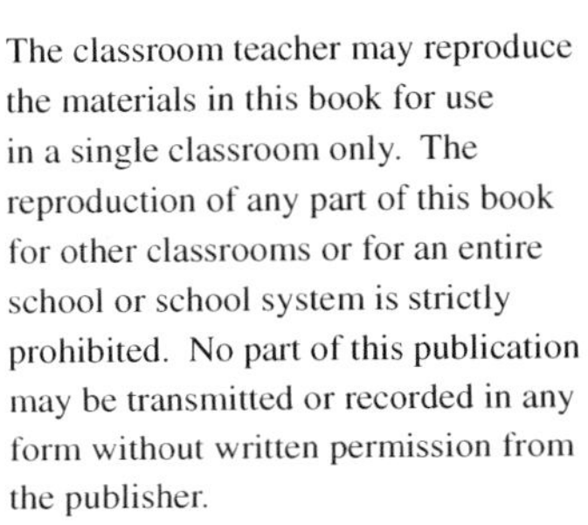

Teacher Created Resources
12621 Western Avenue
Garden Grove, CA 92841
www.teachercreated.com
ISBN: 978-1-4206-8244-1

Teacher Created Resources

Table of Contents

Introduction

Mathematics can be tough for teachers to teach and even tougher for students to learn. Math is not always a fan favorite among the elementary school crowd. It can be intimidating and frustrating. The *Let's Get This Day Started* series is designed to provide students with frequent opportunities to master and retain important math skills in a simple, user-friendly manner.

This book is designed to reinforce key mathematics skills taught in the classroom. As students become active learners in discovering mathematical relationships, they acquire a necessary understanding that improves their problem-solving skills and boosts their confidence in math. When using this book, consider incorporating these activities with the actual curriculum that you may be currently using in your classroom. This provides students with a greater chance of mastering math skills and ultimately being successful in college, career, and life.

The activities in this book do not need to be completed every day or even every other day. Teachers should not feel restricted by a daily warm-up or introductory activity. Sometimes, schedules change. A morning assembly, a make-up lesson, or just an extra-busy day can easily throw off a classroom schedule for days. Teachers never know what their days or weeks are going to look like. This book is written so that teachers can stop wherever and whenever they want. They can take their time and arrange the activities to fit their own schedules. They may choose to do a section a day, or spread it out over a week or two. There is no right or wrong way.

This book is divided into units based on different mathematical-content strands. Each unit consists of activities focused on a topic related to that particular strand. A whole-class introductory sheet kicks off each section, followed by a paired-learning activity sheet, and then an independent-learning assessment. Each section concludes with a written response to a prompt that incorporates the topic studied in the section.

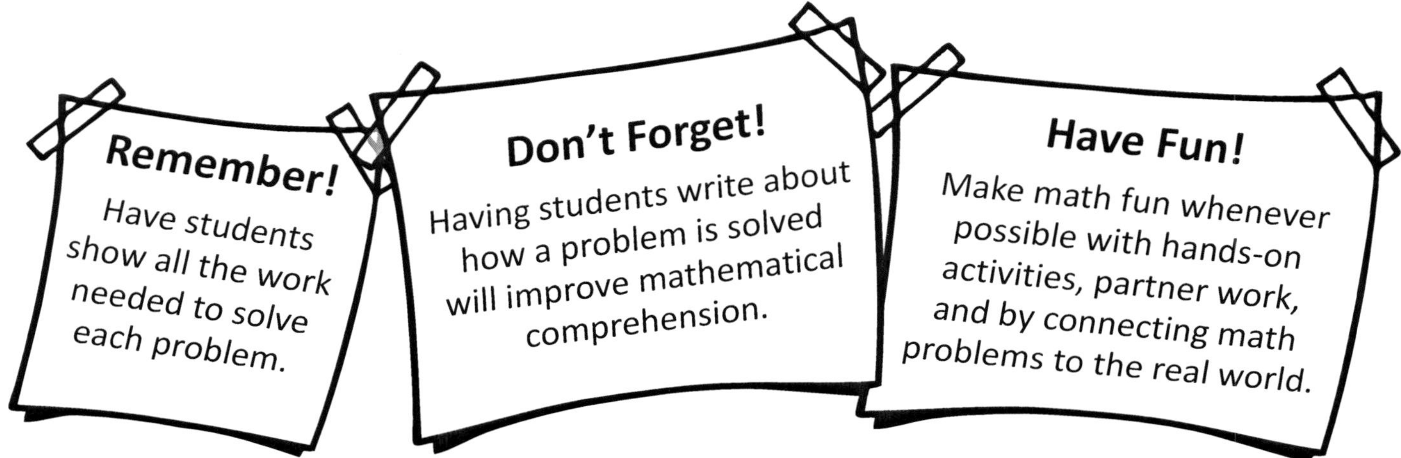
Remember!
Have students show all the work needed to solve each problem.
Don't Forget!
Having students write about how a problem is solved will improve mathematical comprehension.
Have Fun!
Make math fun whenever possible with hands-on activities, partner work, and by connecting math problems to the real world.

All the activities in the *Let's Get This Day Started* series have been aligned to the Common Core State Standards (CCSS). Visit *http://www.teachercreated.com/standards/* for all standards correlations.

How to Use This Book

The first page in each section is the *Read & Learn* page. This page introduces the mathematical topic that will be covered in the section. It breaks down the basics of the mathematical concept by using simple sentences, diagrams, and examples. This page should be a whole-class activity. The teacher should read and review the page with students out loud, answering any questions they may have. These introductory pages can then be saved in a folder and used as study guides, homework helpers, or "cheat sheets."

The second page in each section is the *Partner & Practice* page. This page includes problems for students to solve with a partner. Working collaboratively will provide students with additional guidance and support. Teachers should place students into heterogeneous or homogenous pairs, and circulate around the room as students work together to solve the problems on the page. Teachers should check for understanding and be sure that each student in every pair is actively involved and fully invested in the work. Be sure students show all the work needed to solve each problem. When pairs have finished the page, go over the answers as a class.

The third page in each section is the *Focus & Find* page. This page includes problems for students to solve independently. This page can be completed in class or assigned as homework, and can be used to assess student understanding. Again, be sure students show all the work needed to solve each problem. If students struggle to complete the problems correctly, teachers may choose to supplement with additional learning activities and problems.

The fourth, and final, page in each section is the *Think & Write* page. This page includes writing prompts to help students reflect on the mathematical concept and put their understanding into words. It provides them with opportunities to review, confirm, and reinforce their learning as well as write about how math prolems are solved. Students can save these pages and use them to create a math journal to help them review and study for quizzes and exams.

Read & Learn

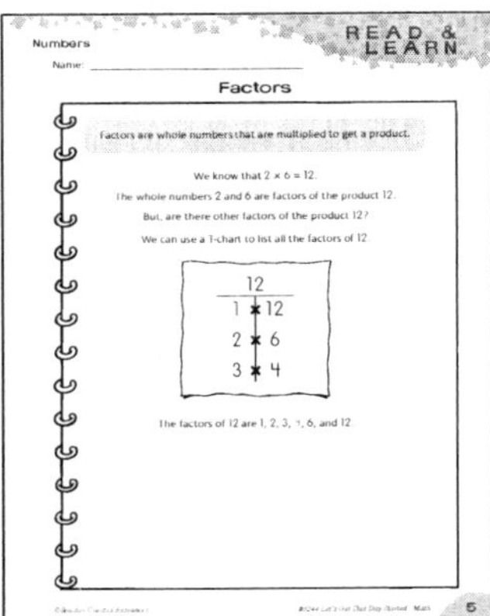

Numbers — READ & LEARN

Name: ____________

Factors

Factors are whole numbers that are multiplied to get a product.

We know that 2 × 6 = 12.

The whole numbers 2 and 6 are factors of the product 12.

But, are there other factors of the product 12?

We can use a T-chart to list all the factors of 12.

12	
1	12
2	6
3	4

The factors of 12 are 1, 2, 3, 4, 6, and 12.

Partner & Practice

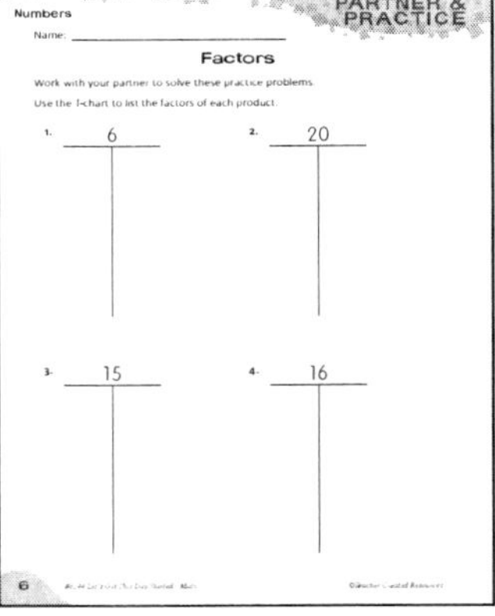

Numbers — PARTNER & PRACTICE

Name: ____________

Factors

Work with your partner to solve these practice problems.

Use the T-chart to list the factors of each product.

1. 6
2. 20
3. 15
4. 16

Focus & Find

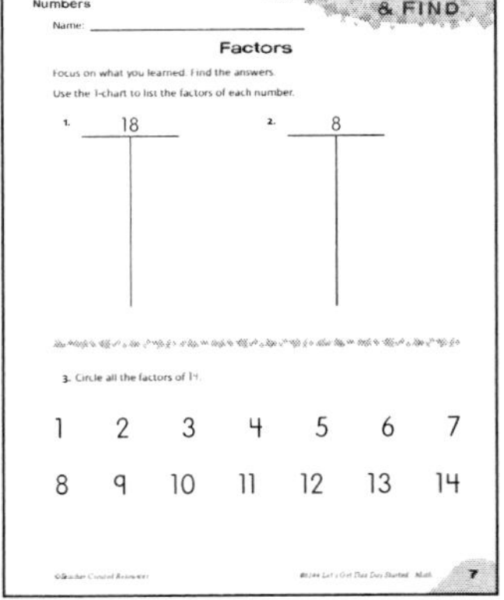

Numbers — FOCUS & FIND

Name: ____________

Factors

Focus on what you learned. Find the answers.

Use the T-chart to list the factors of each number.

1. 18
2. 8

3. Circle all the factors of 14.

1 2 3 4 5 6 7

8 9 10 11 12 13 14

Think & Write

Numbers — THINK & WRITE

Name: ____________

Factors

Think about factors. Write about what you learned.

1. What are factors?
2. What are the factors of 30? How do you know?
3. When I hear someone say factors are fun, I think ____________

Name: ______________________________

Factors

Factors are whole numbers that are multiplied to get a product.

We know that $2 \times 6 = 12$.

The whole numbers 2 and 6 are factors of the product 12.

But, are there other factors of the product 12?

We can use a T-chart to list all the factors of 12.

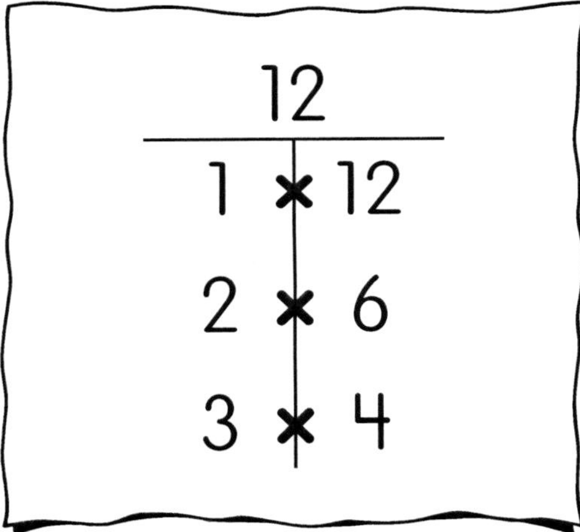

The factors of 12 are 1, 2, 3, 4, 6, and 12.

Name: ______________________________

Factors

Work with your partner to solve these practice problems.

Use the T-chart to list the factors of each product.

1. 6

2. 20

3. 15

4. 16

Name: ____________________________________

Factors

Focus on what you learned. Find the answers.

Use the T-chart to list the factors of each number.

1. 18

2. 8

3. Circle all the factors of 14.

1 2 3 4 5 6 7

8 9 10 11 12 13 14

Name: ______________________________

Factors

Think about factors. Write about what you learned.

1. What are factors?

____

____

____

2. What are the factors of 30? How do you know?

____

____

____

____

3. When I hear someone say factors are fun, I think ______________________________

____

____

____

____

READ & LEARN

Name: ____________________

Prime Numbers & Composite Numbers

We know how to use a T-chart to list the factors of a product.

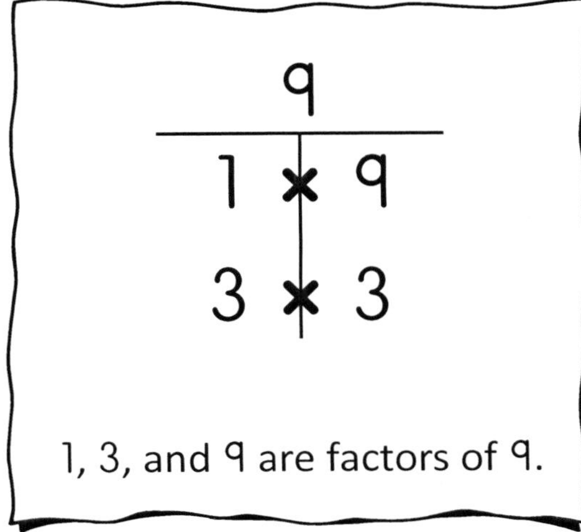

But, how do we know if a number is prime or composite?

Prime Number

A prime number only has one set of factors—1 and itself.

7 is a prime number because its only factors are 1 and 7.

Composite Number

A composite number has more than one set of factors. This means there are other sets of factors besides 1 and itself.

15 is a composite number because $1 \times 15 = 15$ and $3 \times 5 = 15$.

The factors of 15 are 1, 3, 5, and 15.

Name: ______________________________

Prime Numbers & Composite Numbers

Work with your partner to solve these practice problems.

Use a T-chart to list all the factors of each product. Then write whether the number is prime or composite.

1. 11

____

2. 12

____

3. 21

____

4. 29

____

Name: ____________________

Prime Numbers & Composite Numbers

Focus on what you learned. Find the answers.

Write the factors of each number. Then, circle *prime* or *composite*.

1. 9 ____________________

prime composite

2. 14 ____________________

prime composite

3. 17 ____________________

prime composite

4. 16 ____________________

prime composite

5. 10 ____________________

prime composite

6. 13 ____________________

prime composite

7. List three prime numbers.

____

8. List three composite numbers.

____

Name: ______________________________

Prime Numbers & Composite Numbers

Think about prime and composite numbers. Write about what you learned.

1. What is the difference between prime and composite numbers?

____

____

____

2. Is 15 a prime or composite number? How do you know?

____

____

____

____

3. I feel (confident/confused) about prime and composite numbers because

____

____

____

____

Name: ______________________________

Number Patterns

We know how to make patterns with shapes or objects.

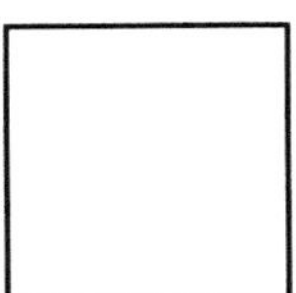 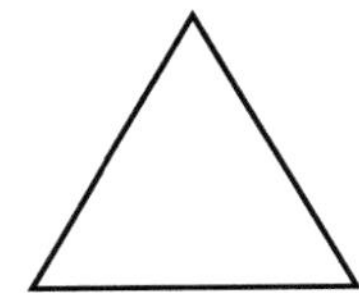 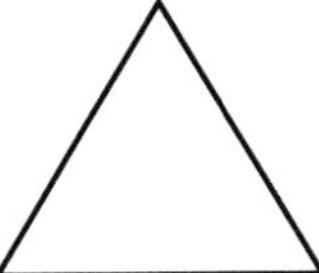  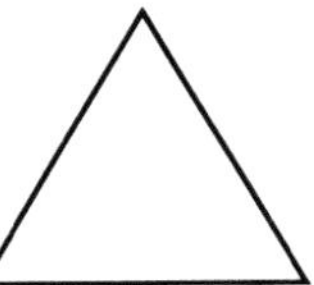 

We can also make number patterns with a given rule.

For example, we can make a number pattern with the rule "add 2."

1, 3, 5, 7, 9, 11

(1 + 2 = 3; 3 + 2 = 5; 5 + 2 = 7; 7 +2 = 9; 9 + 2 = 11)

Sometimes we do not know the rule of the pattern. But we can look closely at the numbers to find the pattern's rule.

5, 11, 17, 23, 29

The rule of this pattern is "add 6."

(5 + 6 = 11; 11 + 6 = 17; 17 + 6 = 23; 23 + 6 = 29)

Name: ________________________________

Number Patterns

Work with your partner to solve these practice problems.

1. Write the next two numbers of the pattern, using the rule "Add 4."

   3, 7, 11, 15, ________, ________

2. Write the next two numbers of the pattern, using the rule "Add 5."

   4, 9, 14, 19, ________, ________

Find the rule of each pattern. Then, write the next two numbers in the pattern.

3. 2, 4, 8, 16, ________, ________

   Rule: ____________________________

4. 1, 4, 7, 10, ________, ________

   Rule: ____________________________

Name: ______________________________

Number Patterns

Focus on what you learned. Find the answers.

Write two numbers to continue each pattern. Write the rule for each pattern.

1. 0, 3, 6, 9, ________, ________

   Rule: ______________________

2. 12, 22, 32, 42, ________, ________

   Rule: ______________________

3. 14, 21, 28, 35, ________, ________

   Rule: ______________________

4. 21, 19, 17, 15, ________, ________

   Rule: ______________________

Name: ______________________________

Number Patterns

Think about number patterns. Write about what you learned.

1. What do you notice about number patterns?

____

____

____

____

2. What is the rule for the pattern? How do you know?

1, 3, 9, 27, 81, 243

____

____

____

____

3. I want to become better at number patterns, so I will ______________________________

____

____

____

READ & LEARN

Name: ______________________________

Rounding Numbers

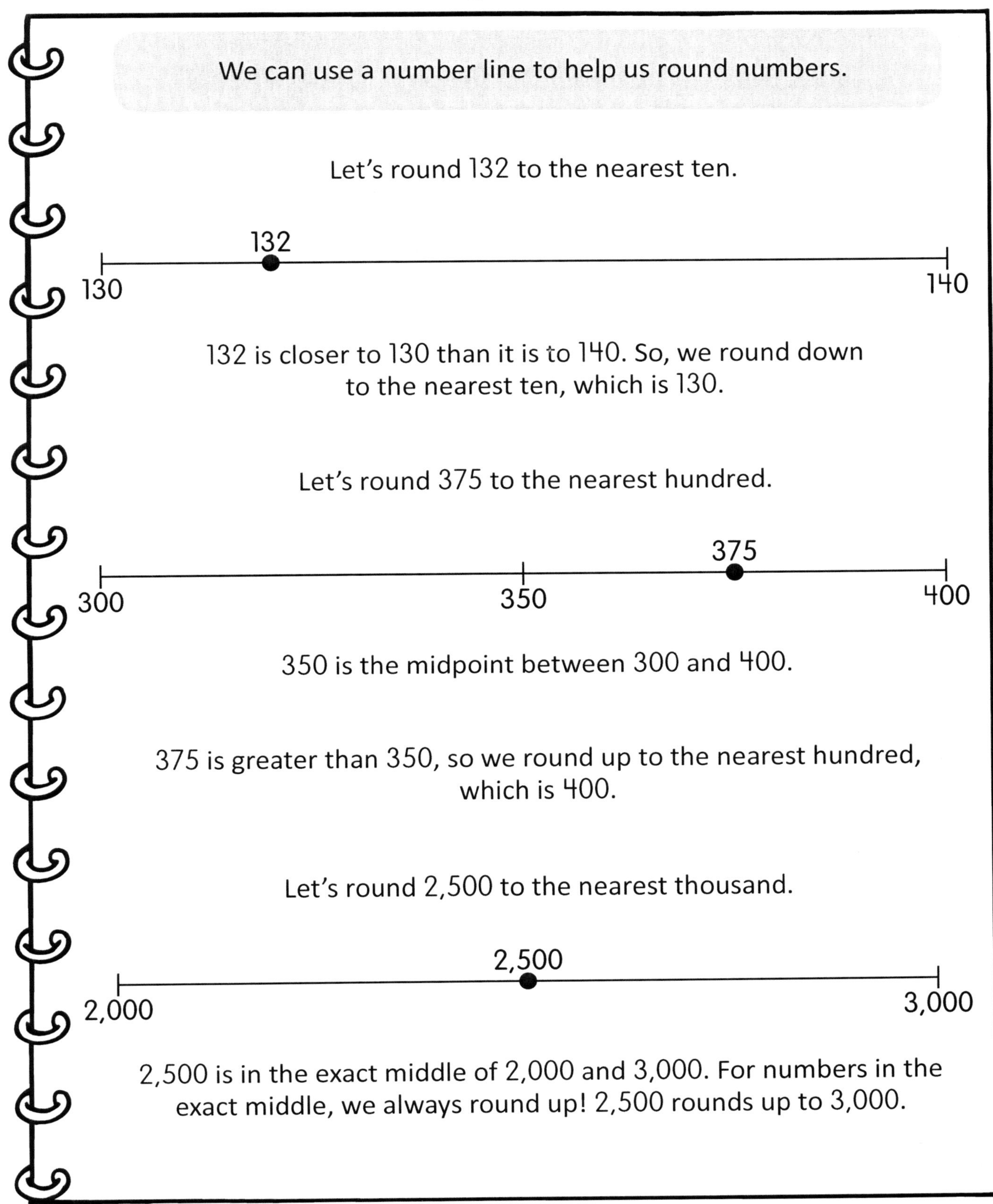

We can use a number line to help us round numbers.
Let's round 132 to the nearest ten.
132
130
140
132 is closer to 130 than it is to 140. So, we round down to the nearest ten, which is 130.
Let's round 375 to the nearest hundred.
375
300
350
400
350 is the midpoint between 300 and 400.
375 is greater than 350, so we round up to the nearest hundred, which is 400.
Let's round 2,500 to the nearest thousand.
2,500
2,000
3,000
2,500 is in the exact middle of 2,000 and 3,000. For numbers in the exact middle, we always round up! 2,500 rounds up to 3,000.

Name: ______________________________

Rounding Numbers

Work with your partner to solve these practice problems.

1. Use the number line to round 346 to the nearest hundred.

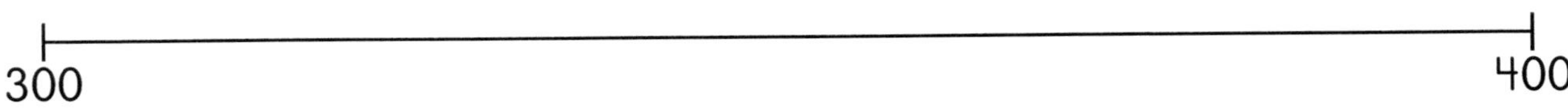

____

2. Use the number line to round 1,536 to the nearest ten.

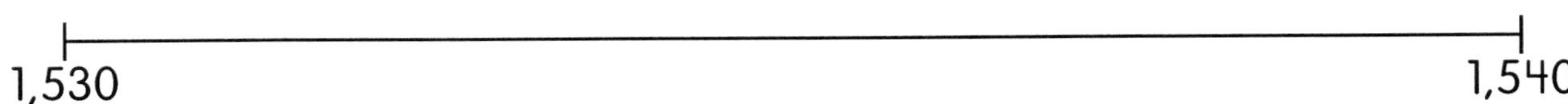

____

FOCUS & FIND

Name: ______________________

Rounding Numbers

Focus on what you learned. Find the answers.

Round to the nearest ten. Use the number line to help you.

1. 312 __________
2. 561 __________

Round to the nearest hundred. Use the number line to help you.

3. 561 __________
4. 1,225 __________

Round to the nearest thousand. Use the number line to help you.

5. 5,689 __________
6. 1,278 __________

Name: ______________________________

Rounding Numbers

Think about rounding numbers. Write about what you learned.

1. How can a number line help you round numbers?

____

____

____

2. What is 2,345 rounded to the nearest ten? How do you know?

____

____

____

____

3. The most important thing to remember about rounding numbers is __________

____

____

____

READ & LEARN

Name: ______________________________

Comparing Numbers

We can use what we know about place value and numbers to compare two numbers.

When we compare numbers, we use three symbols.

$>$	$<$	$=$
greater than	less than	equal to

Working from left to right, we use place value to compare a set of numbers.

1,257 (?) 1,243

Both numbers have a 1 in the thousands place.

1,257 (?) 1,243

Both numbers have a 2 in the hundreds place.

1,257 (?) 1,243

But, the first number has a 5 in the tens place,

while the second number has a 4 in the tens place.

1,257 (?) 1,243

5 tens is greater than 4 tens.

Therefore, 1,257 is greater than 1,243.

1,257 $>$ 1,243

Name: ____________________________

Comparing Numbers

Work with your partner to solve these practice problems.

Write >, <, or = to compare each set of numbers.

1. 578 ◯ 5,078
2. 499 ◯ 374
3. 2,347 ◯ 2,341
4. 853 ◯ 853
5. 1,750 ◯ 1,753
6. 4,672 ◯ 467
7. 978 ◯ 987
8. 3,001 ◯ 3,010

Name: ______________________________

Comparing Numbers

Focus on what you learned. Find the answers.

Write >, <, or = to compare each set of numbers.

1. 514 ◯ 541
2. 2,101 ◯ 2,011
3. 942 ◯ 9,042
4. 2,151 ◯ 1,251

Write a number to complete each comparison.

5. 1,782 > ________
6. 427 < ________
7. 9,812 = ________
8. 521 > ________

Name: ________________________________

Comparing Numbers

Think about comparing numbers. Write about what you learned.

1. What symbols are used to compare numbers? Explain what each symbol means.

____

____

____

2. Which number is greater? How do you know?

1,345 ◯ 1,354

____

____

____

____

3. When I think of comparing numbers, I think ______________________

____

____

____

Name: ____________________

Adding Multi-Digit Numbers

We know how to add two-digit and three-digit numbers with and without regrouping.

$$\begin{array}{r} \overset{1}{5}72 \\ +\ 81 \\ \hline 653 \end{array}$$

with regrouping

$$\begin{array}{r} 45 \\ +12 \\ \hline 57 \end{array}$$

without regrouping

We can use what we know to add multi-digit numbers.

$$\begin{array}{r} \overset{1}{5},\overset{1}{7}81 \\ +\ 1,522 \\ \hline 7,303 \end{array}$$

with regrouping

$$\begin{array}{r} 9,246 \\ +\ 501 \\ \hline 9,747 \end{array}$$

without regrouping

Remember!
Start with the ones place, and work your way left to the last digit.

Name: ____________________________________

Adding Multi-Digit Numbers

Work with your partner to solve these practice problems.

1.
$$\begin{array}{r} 5{,}722 \\ +\ 1{,}341 \\ \hline 7{,}063 \end{array}$$

2.
$$\begin{array}{r} 2{,}981 \\ +\ \quad 511 \\ \hline 3{,}492 \end{array}$$

3.
$$\begin{array}{r} 8{,}518 \\ +\ 1{,}002 \\ \hline 9{,}520 \end{array}$$

4.
$$\begin{array}{r} 7{,}542 \\ +\ \quad 135 \\ \hline 7{,}677 \end{array}$$

5.
$$\begin{array}{r} 7{,}001 \\ +\ 2{,}115 \\ \hline 9{,}116 \end{array}$$

6.
$$\begin{array}{r} 3{,}582 \\ +\ 1{,}509 \\ \hline 5{,}091 \end{array}$$

Name: ______________________________

Adding Multi-Digit Numbers

Focus on what you learned. Find the answers.

1.
$$\begin{array}{r} 4{,}307 \\ +\ 1{,}245 \\ \hline 5{,}553 \end{array}$$

2.
$$\begin{array}{r} 9{,}389 \\ +\ 356 \\ \hline 9{,}745 \end{array}$$

3.
$$\begin{array}{r} 2{,}305 \\ +\ 5{,}230 \\ \hline 7{,}535 \end{array}$$

4.
$$\begin{array}{r} 7{,}620 \\ +\ 1{,}250 \\ \hline 8{,}870 \end{array}$$

5.
$$\begin{array}{r} 3{,}475 \\ +\ 948 \\ \hline 4{,}423 \end{array}$$

6.
$$\begin{array}{r} 6{,}229 \\ +\ 2{,}471 \\ \hline 8{,}700 \end{array}$$

Name: ______________________________

Adding Multi-Digit Numbers

Think about adding multi-digit numbers. Write about what you learned.

1. Write an addition problem that uses regrouping. Then, solve your problem.

2. What is 1,672 + 299? Explain how you solved this problem.

____

____

____

____

3. Write about a time you had to add multi-digit numbers in the real world.

____

____

____

____

Name: ______________________________

Subtracting Multi-Digit Numbers

We can use what we know about subtracting numbers to subtract multi-digit numbers.

$$\begin{array}{r} 5{,}829 \\ -\ 1{,}703 \\ \hline 4{,}126 \end{array}$$

Sometimes, we have to regroup before we can subtract.

Regroup one thousand into 10 hundreds. →

$$\begin{array}{r} \overset{1}{\cancel{2}},\overset{11}{\cancel{1}}90 \\ -\ \ \ 870 \\ \hline 1{,}320 \end{array}$$

We can follow these steps to subtract numbers with any amount of digits.

Name: ______________________________

Subtracting Multi-Digit Numbers

Work with your partner to solve these practice problems.

1. 9,295 − 5,234 = 4,061

2. 8,001 − 500 = 7,501

3. 7,522 − 4,170 = 3,352

4. 4,872 − 3,954 = 0818

5. 1,528 − 434 = 1,094

6. 6,529 − 1,367 = 5,162

Name: ____________________________

Subtracting Multi-Digit Numbers

Focus on what you learned. Find the answers.

1. $\begin{array}{r} 3{,}456 \\ -\ 1{,}238 \\ \hline \end{array}$

   2,218

2. $\begin{array}{r} 5{,}390 \\ -\ 937 \\ \hline \end{array}$

   4,453

3. $\begin{array}{r} 9{,}200 \\ -\ 4{,}378 \\ \hline \end{array}$

   4,822

4. $\begin{array}{r} 3{,}598 \\ -\ 2{,}500 \\ \hline \end{array}$

   1,098

5. $\begin{array}{r} 2{,}009 \\ -\ 1{,}478 \\ \hline \end{array}$

   0531

6. $\begin{array}{r} 4{,}830 \\ -\ 1{,}321 \\ \hline \end{array}$

   3,509

Name: ______________________________

Subtracting Multi-digit Numbers

Think about subtracting multi-digit numbers. Write about what you learned.

1. Write a subtraction problem that needs regrouping. Then, solve your problem.

2. What is 2,894 – 256? How do you know? Explain your steps.

____

____

____

____

3. I use subtraction in my life when I ______________________________

____

____

____

Name: ____________________

Multiplying by One-Digit Numbers

We can use what we know to multiply larger numbers by one-digit numbers.

Let's try!

$$721 \times 3$$

First, we can break apart the larger number into expanded form.

$$700 + 20 + 1$$

With this strategy we are multiplying 700×3, 20×3, and 1×3.

Next, we can find the product of each one.

$$\begin{array}{r} 700 \\ \times \quad 3 \\ \hline 2{,}100 \end{array} \qquad \begin{array}{r} 20 \\ \times \quad 3 \\ \hline 60 \end{array} \qquad \begin{array}{r} 1 \\ \times 3 \\ \hline 3 \end{array}$$

Then, we can add them together to find the answer.

$$\begin{array}{r} 2{,}100 \\ 60 \\ + \quad 3 \\ \hline 2{,}163 \end{array}$$

$$721 \times 3 = 2{,}163$$

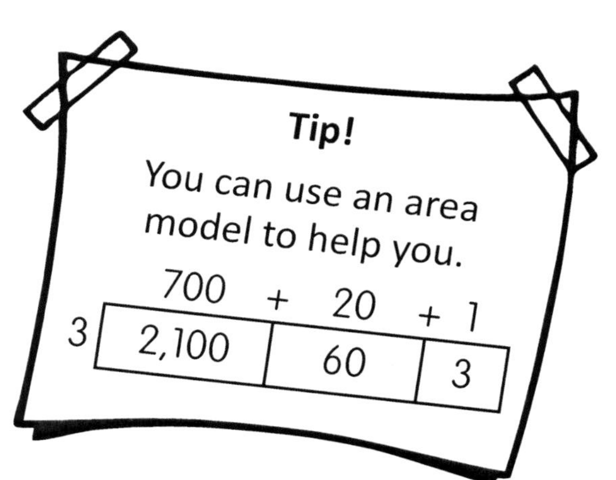
Tip!
You can use an area model to help you.
700 + 20 + 1
3
2,100
60
3

Name: ______________________

Multiplying by One-Digit Numbers

Work with your partner to solve these practice problems.

Use the area model to multiply.

1. $856 \times 2 =$ __________

800 + 50 + 6

2

2. $1{,}525 \times 4 =$ __________

1,000 + 500 + 20 + 5

4

3. $2{,}688 \times 5 =$ __________

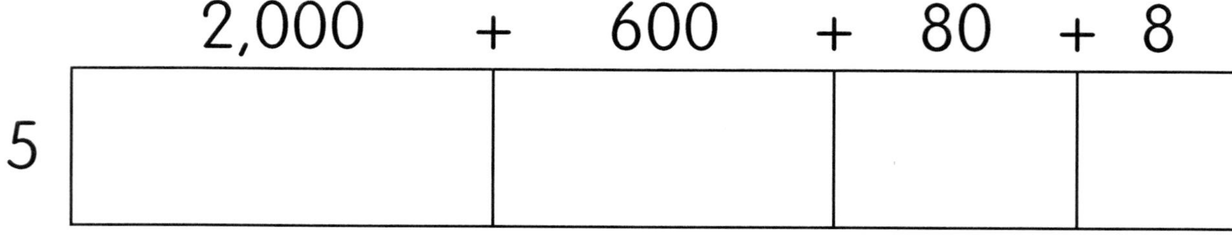

Name: ______________________________

Multiplying by One-Digit Numbers

Focus on what you learned. Find the answers.

Complete the area model to solve each problem.

1. $5{,}671 \times 2 =$ ____________

2. $980 \times 6 =$ ____________

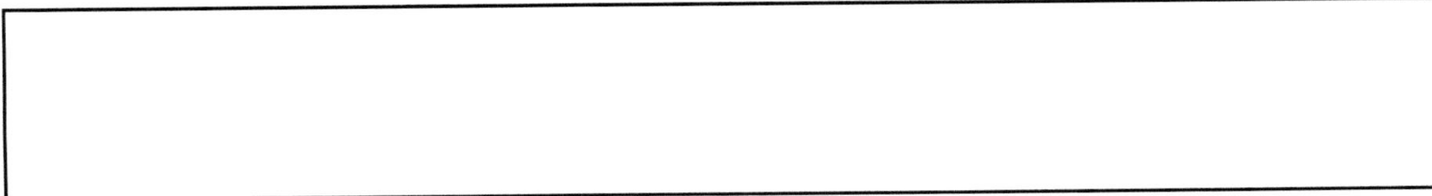

3. $4{,}201 \times 3 =$ ____________

Name: ______________________________

Multiplying by One-Digit Numbers

Think about multiplying by one-digit numbers. Write about what you learned.

1. How does an area model help you multiply?

____

____

____

____

2. What is the product of $1{,}824 \times 5$? How do you know?

____

____

____

3. I want to become better at multiplying by one-digit numbers, so I will ________

____

____

____

Name: ______________________________

Multiplying by Two-Digit Numbers

We know how to use an area model to multiply four-digit numbers by one-digit numbers.

$$1{,}629 \times 3$$

	1,000	+ 600	+ 20	+ 9
3	3,000	1,800	60	27

$$\begin{array}{r} 3{,}000 \\ 1{,}800 \\ 60 \\ +\quad 27 \\ \hline 4{,}887 \end{array}$$

$$1{,}629 \times 3 = 4{,}887$$

We can also use an area model to multiply two two-digit numbers.

Let's try!

$$23 \times 15$$

×	20	+ 3
10	200	30
+ 5	100	15

$$\begin{array}{rr} 20 \times 10 = & 200 \\ 20 \times 5 = & 100 \\ 10 \times 3 = & 30 \\ 5 \times 3 = & +\quad 15 \\ \hline & 345 \end{array}$$

$$23 \times 15 = 345$$

Name: ______________________________

Multiplying by Two-Digit Numbers

Work with your partner to solve these practice problems.

1. $18 \times 26 =$ ________

×	10	8
20		
6		

2. $37 \times 12 =$ ________

×	30	7
10		
2		

3. $27 \times 31 =$ ________

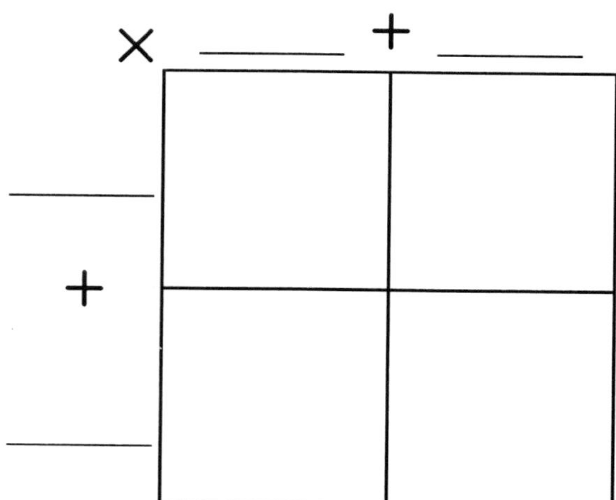

4. $61 \times 15 =$ ________

×	____	____
____		
____		

Name: ______________________________

Multiplying by Two-Digit Numbers

Focus on what you learned. Find the answers.

1. $42 \times 16 =$ ________

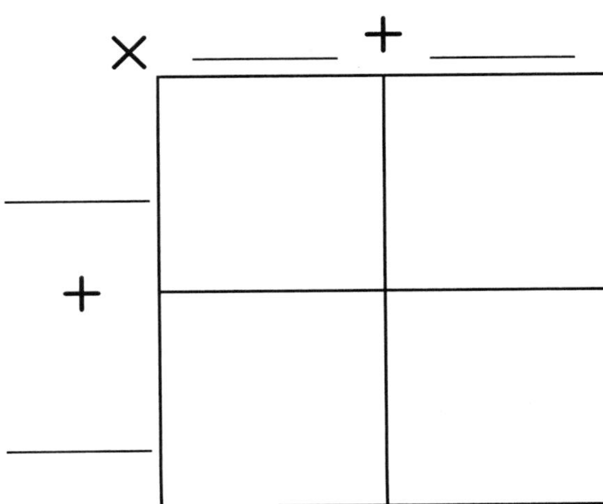

2. $53 \times 41 =$ ________

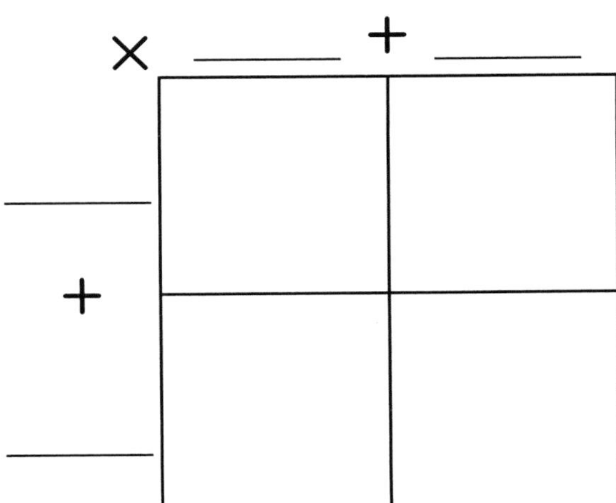

3. $38 \times 29 =$ ________

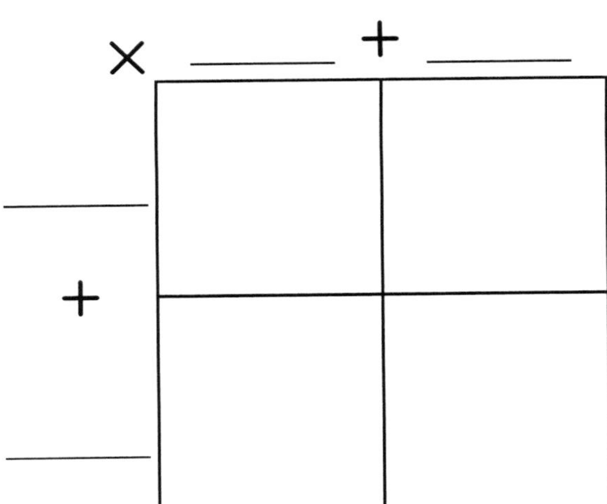

4. $62 \times 13 =$ ________

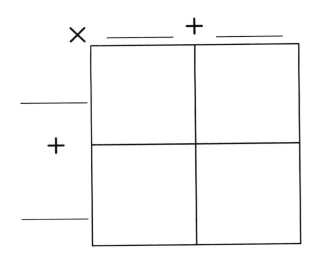

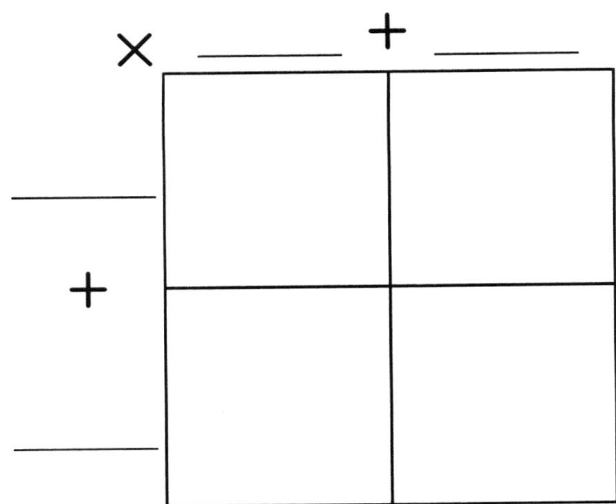

Name: ____________________

Multiplying by Two-Digit Numbers

Think about multiplying by two-digit numbers. Write about what you learned.

1. How does an area model help you multiply two two-digit numbers?

I'm not sure because we did not lean it in shool this year but my guess is that it gives a visual exampe.

2. Which is the correct answer for 25 × 17? How do you know?

425 415

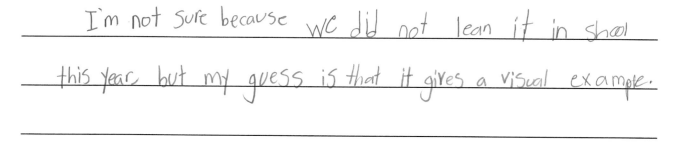

I know because I multiplied

$$\begin{array}{r} 25 \\ \times 17 \\ \hline 175 \\ 250 \\ \hline 425 \end{array}$$

3. When I think of multiplying two two-digit numbers, I feel like i'm doing math. If you were looking for a different kind of answer, then I feel confedent.

Name: ______________________________

READ & LEARN

Dividing Large Numbers

How do we divide large numbers? We can use an area model and break down the dividend into easily divisible numbers.

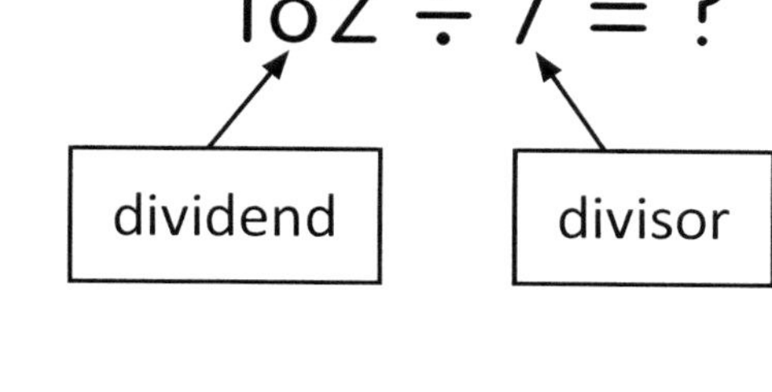

Subtract 140 from 182.

$$\begin{array}{r} 182 \\ -140 \\ \hline 42 \\ -42 \\ \hline 0 \end{array}$$

no remainder

×	20	
7	140	42

140 is easily divisible by 7.

$20 \times 7 = 140$

$7 \times 6 = 42$

×	20	+ 6
7	140	42

Add the partial quotients:

$$20 + 6 = 26$$

$$182 \div 7 = 26$$

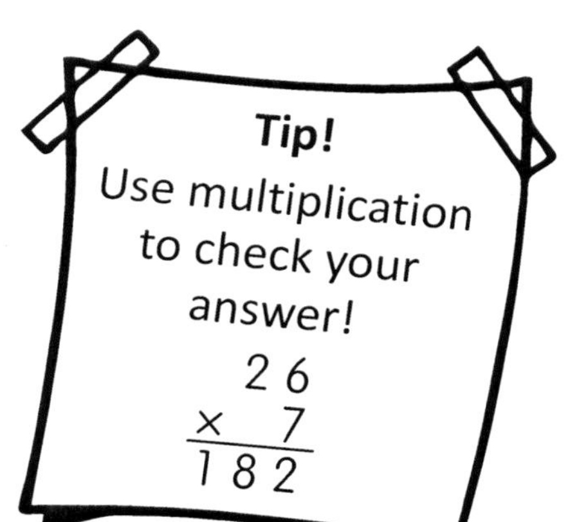

Name: ______________________________

Dividing Large Numbers

Work with your partner to solve these practice problems.

1. 126 ÷ 3 = 42

3 | 126 (42)

3 | ______________________________ |

4 | 144 (36)

2. 144 ÷ 4 = 36

4 | ______________________________ |

8 | 464 (58)

3. 464 ÷ 8 = 58

8 | ______________________________ |

FOCUS & FIND

Name: ____________________________

Dividing Large Numbers

Focus on what you learned. Find the answers.

1. 648 ÷ 9 = 72

9 [ ]

2. 136 ÷ 8 = 17

8 [ ]

3. 215 ÷ 5 = 43

5 [ ]

Name: ______________________________

Dividing Large Numbers

Think about dividing large numbers. Write about what you learned.

1. What are partial quotients? How do they help you divide large numbers?

____

____

____

____

2. How can you check your answers to division problems?

____

____

____

3. When I hear someone say that dividing large numbers is fun, I think __________

____

____

____

Name: ______________________________

Equivalent Fractions

We know that fractions are part of a whole.

$\frac{1}{4}$

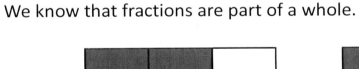

$\frac{2}{6}$

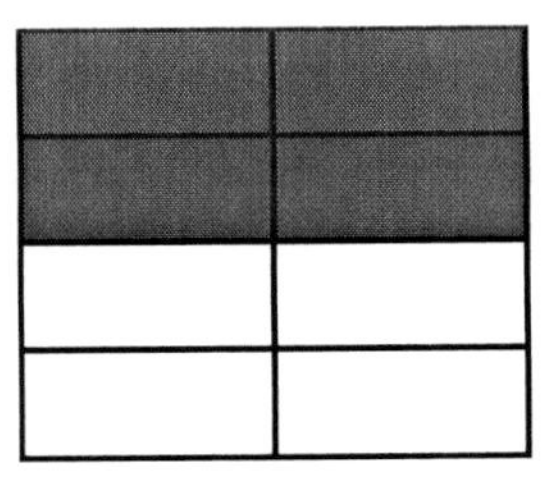

$\frac{1}{2}$

Equivalent fractions are fractions that take up the same amount of space within the whole. The whole must be the exact same size to be able to find equivalent fractions.

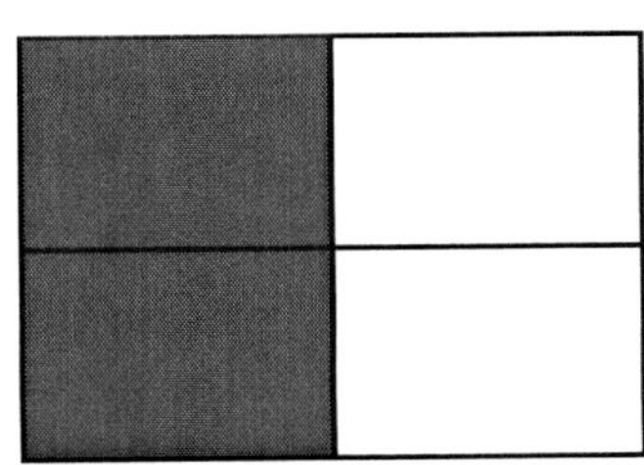

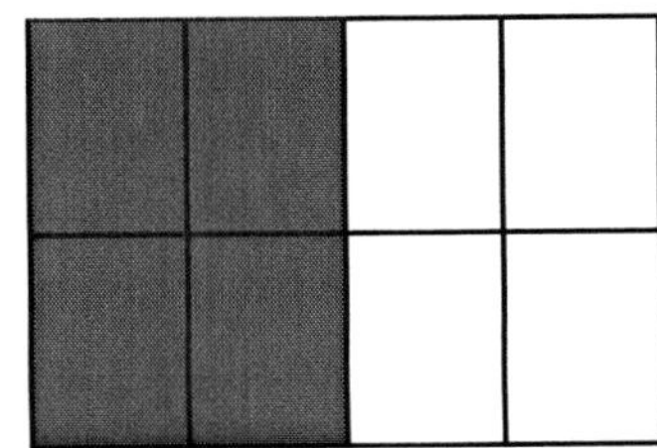

$\frac{2}{4} = \frac{4}{8}$

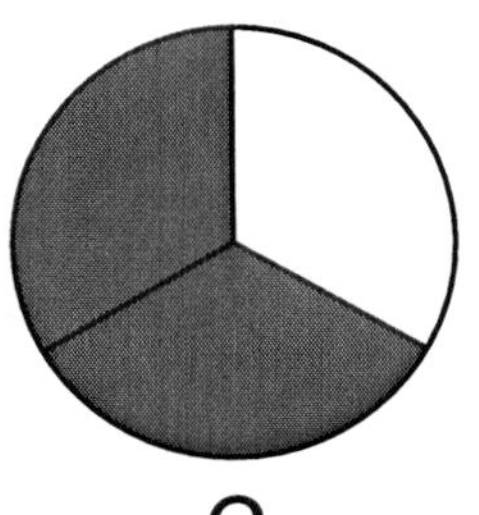

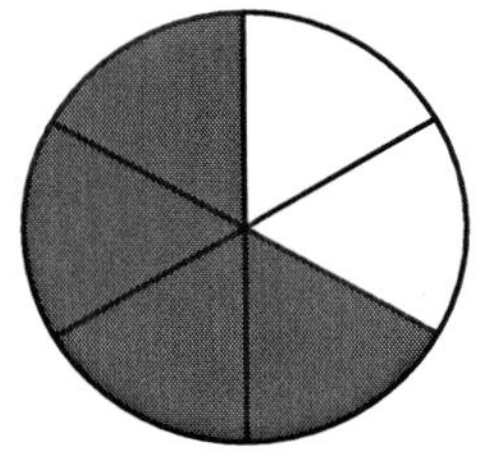

$\frac{2}{3} = \frac{4}{6}$

PARTNER & PRACTICE

Name: ______________________________

Equivalent Fractions

Work with your partner to solve these practice problems.

Shade to find an equivalent fraction for each given fraction.

1.

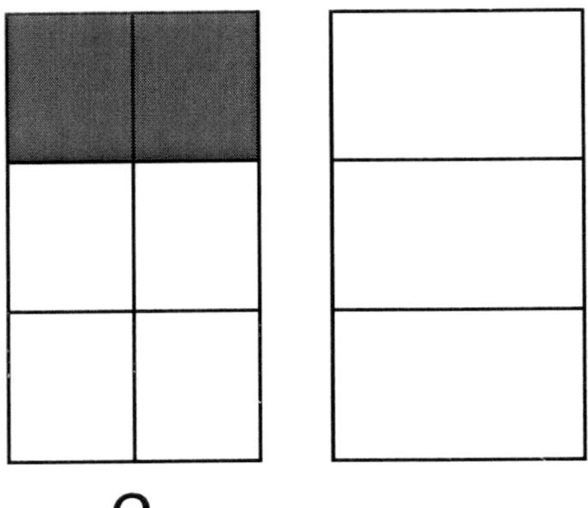

$\frac{2}{6} = \frac{}{3}$

2.

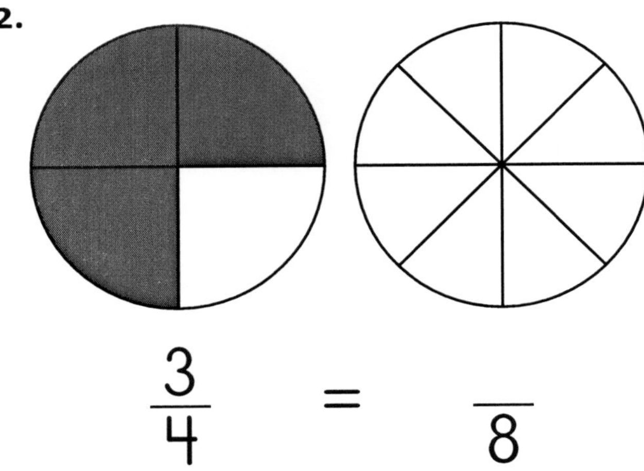

$\frac{3}{4} = \frac{}{8}$

3.

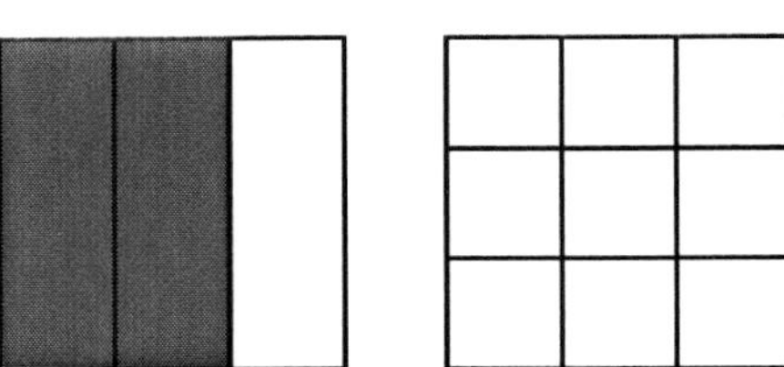

$\frac{2}{3} = \frac{}{9}$

4.

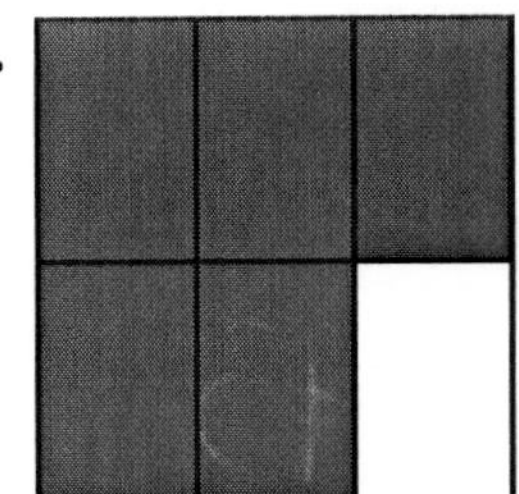 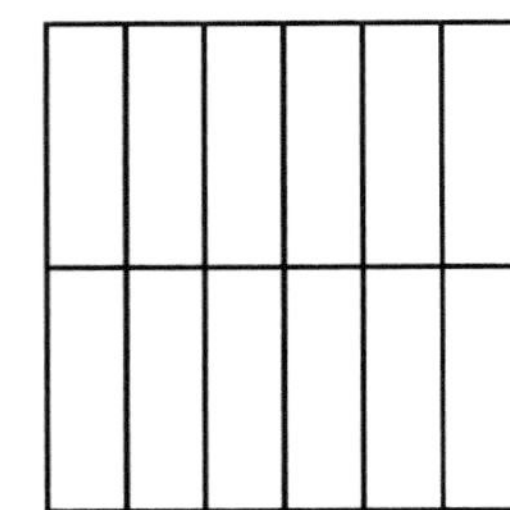

$\frac{5}{6} = \frac{}{12}$

FOCUS & FIND

Name: ______________________________

Equivalent Fractions

Focus on what you learned. Find the answers.

Write an equivalent fraction for each given fraction. Draw a picture to help you.

1. $\frac{1}{2} = \frac{\quad}{4}$

2. $\frac{3}{6} = \frac{\quad}{12}$

3. $\frac{4}{6} = \frac{\quad}{3}$

4. $\frac{2}{8} = \frac{\quad}{4}$

5. $\frac{3}{4} = \frac{\quad}{8}$

6. $\frac{4}{6} = \frac{\quad}{12}$

7. $\frac{3}{6} = \frac{\quad}{4}$

8. $\frac{3}{5} = \frac{\quad}{10}$

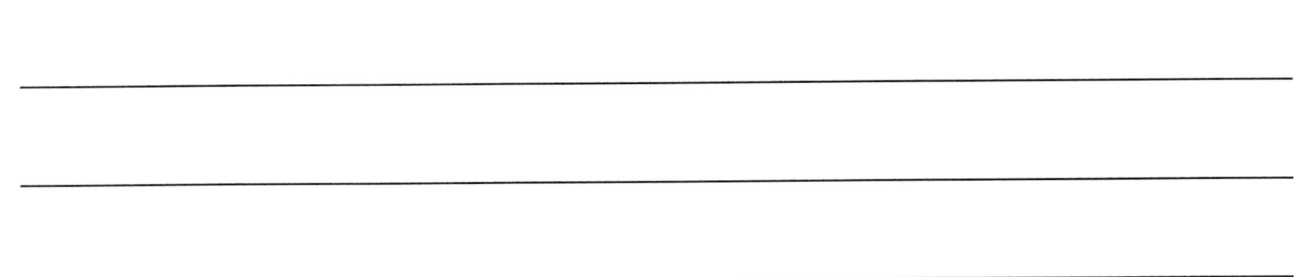

Name: ___________________________

Equivalent Fractions

Think about equivalent fractions. Write about what you learned.

1. What makes two fractions equivalent?

____

____

____

2. Do the pictures represent equivalent fractions? How do you know?

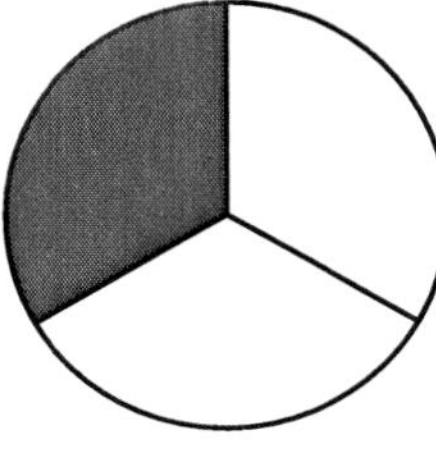

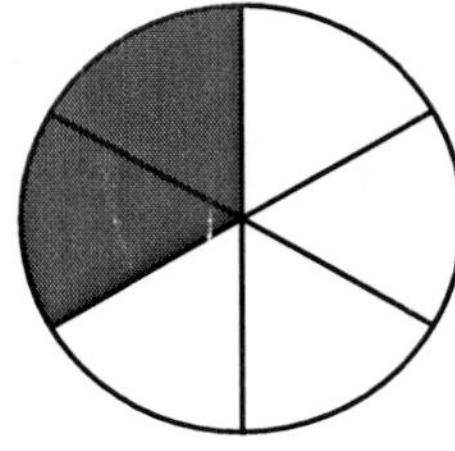

____

____

____

____

3. Equivalent fractions are (fun/easy/difficult) because _______________

____

____

____

Name: ______________________________

Comparing Fractions

We know how to find equivalent fractions.

We use the equal sign (=) to show equivalent fractions.

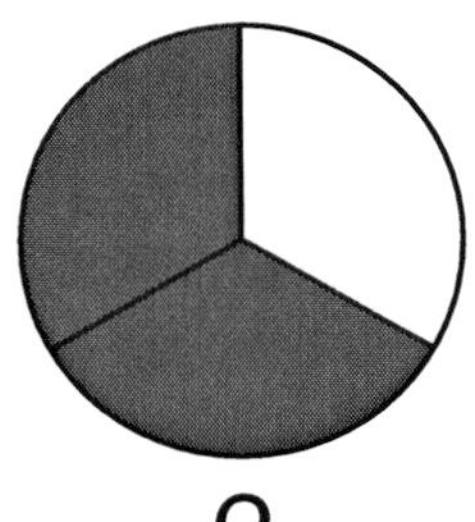

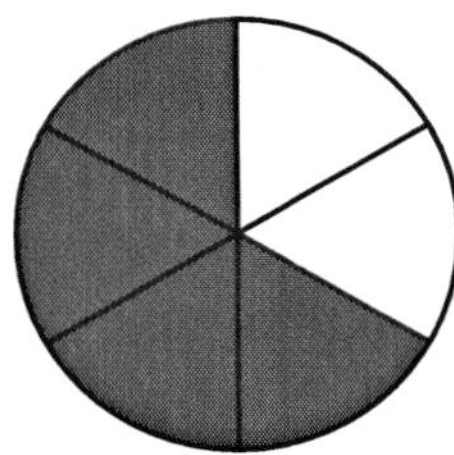

$\frac{2}{3} = \frac{4}{6}$

But, how do we compare fractions that are not equivalent?

We decide whether a fraction is greater than (>) or less than (<) another fraction.

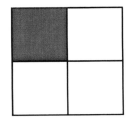

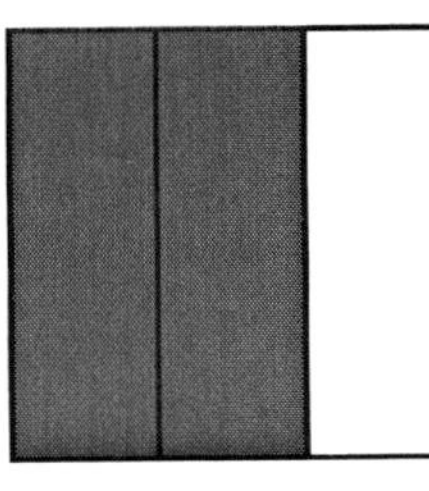

$\frac{2}{3} > \frac{1}{4}$

Remember!

We can only compare fractions when they refer to the same whole.

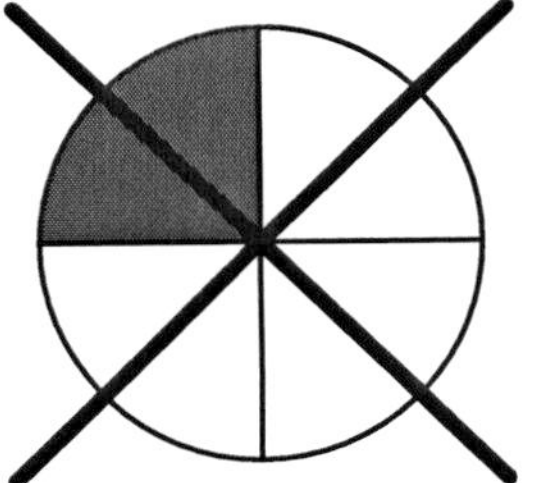

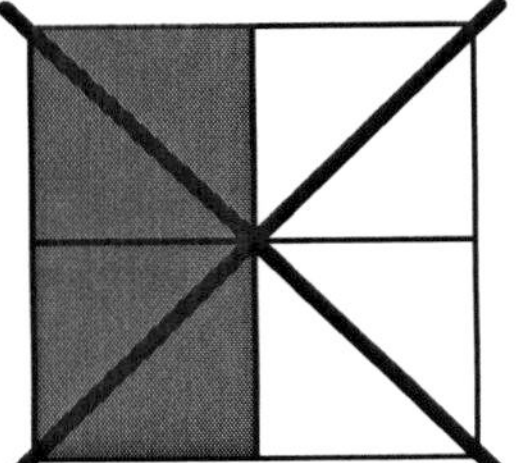

Name: ____________________

Comparing Fractions

Work with your partner to solve these practice problems.

Compare the fractions. Write >, <, or =.

1. 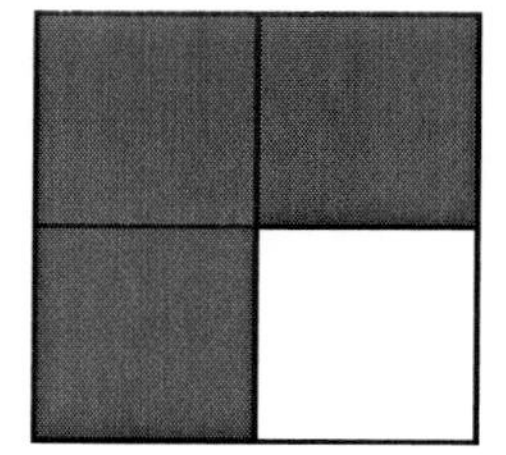 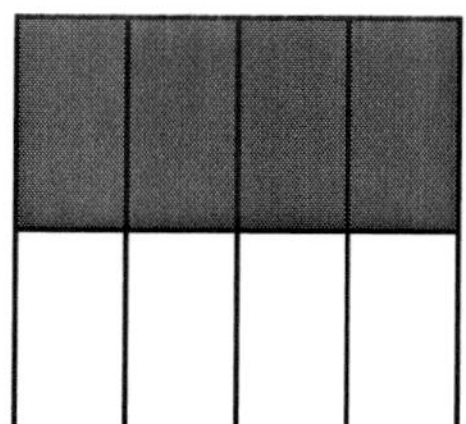

$\frac{3}{4}$ 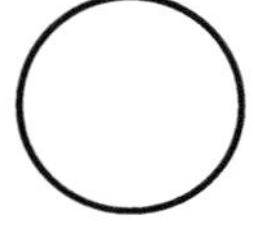 $\frac{4}{8}$

2. 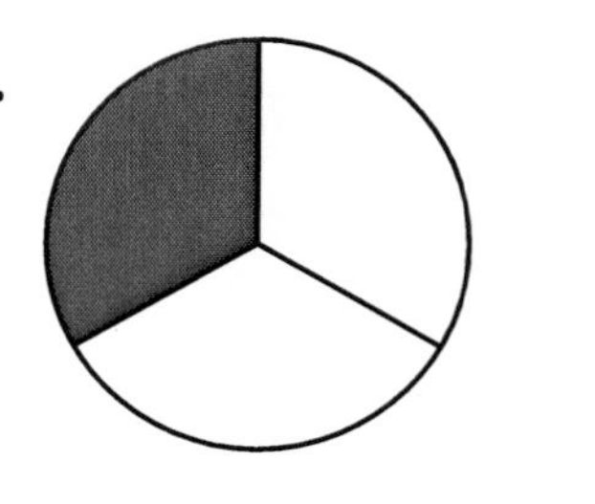 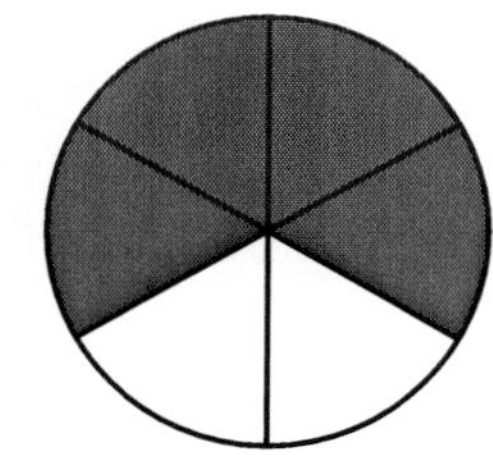

$\frac{1}{3}$ 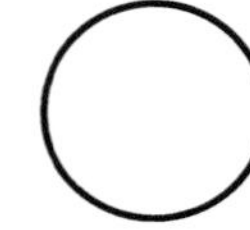 $\frac{4}{6}$

3. 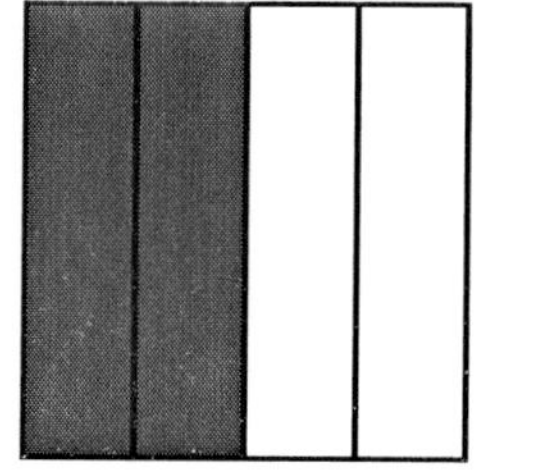

$\frac{2}{4}$  $\frac{2}{3}$

4. 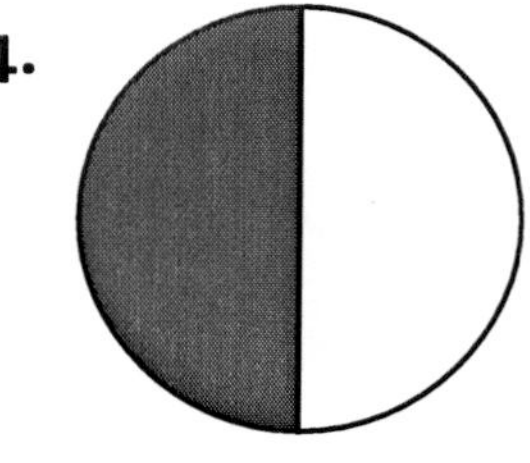

$\frac{1}{2}$  $\frac{2}{8}$

5. $\frac{1}{5}$ ◯ $\frac{1}{6}$

6. $\frac{1}{2}$ ◯ $\frac{2}{3}$

Name: ________________________________

Comparing Fractions

Focus on what you learned. Find the answers.

Write >, <, or = to compare the fractions.

1. $\frac{2}{3}$ ◯ $\frac{1}{4}$

2. $\frac{1}{8}$ ◯ $\frac{1}{5}$

3. $\frac{2}{4}$ ◯ $\frac{1}{2}$

4. $\frac{2}{5}$ ◯ $\frac{2}{3}$

5. $\frac{7}{10}$ ◯ $\frac{6}{10}$

6. $\frac{3}{6}$ ◯ $\frac{4}{8}$

7. $\frac{3}{5}$ ◯ $\frac{3}{4}$

8. $\frac{2}{10}$ ◯ $\frac{2}{8}$

THINK & WRITE

Name: ______________________________

Comparing Fractions

Think about comparing fractions. Write about what you learned.

1. What does it mean to compare fractions?

____

____

____

2. Is the inequality true? How do you know?

$$\frac{2}{3} > \frac{1}{4}$$

____

____

____

____

3. Write about a situation in the real world where you may have to compare fractions.

____

____

____

____

Name: ______________________________

Adding Mixed Numbers with Like Denominators

A mixed number contains a whole number and a fraction.

For example, the mixed number $2\frac{1}{2}$ represents 2 wholes and $\frac{1}{2}$ of a whole, or $2 + \frac{1}{2}$.

$2\frac{1}{2}$ 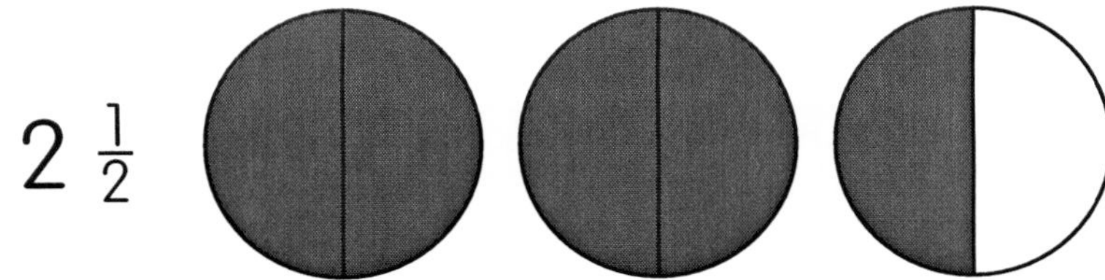

We can add mixed numbers.

$$3\frac{3}{5} + 2\frac{1}{5}$$

First, we add the whole numbers.

$$\boxed{3}\frac{3}{5} + \boxed{2}\frac{1}{5}$$

$$3 + 2 = \textcircled{5}$$

Then, we add the fraction parts.

$$3\boxed{\frac{3}{5}} + 2\boxed{\frac{1}{5}}$$

$$\frac{3}{5} + \frac{1}{5} = \textcircled{\frac{4}{5}}$$

$$3\frac{3}{5} + 2\frac{1}{5} = 5\frac{4}{5}$$

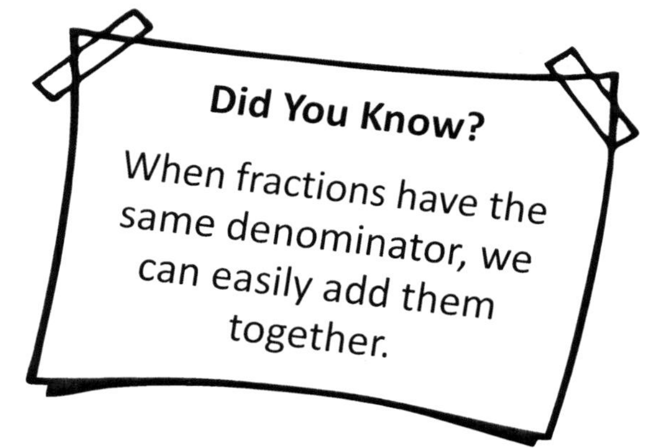
Did You Know?
When fractions have the same denominator, we can easily add them together.

Name: ______________________________

Adding Mixed Numbers with Like Denominators

Work with your partner to solve these practice problems.

1. $3\frac{1}{4} + 6\frac{1}{4} =$ ________

2. $2\frac{1}{3} + 2\frac{1}{3} =$ ________

3. $10\frac{1}{2} + 1\frac{1}{2} =$ ________

4. $5\frac{3}{4} + 1\frac{1}{4} =$ ________

5. $2\frac{1}{6} + 4\frac{2}{6} =$ ________

6. $1\frac{2}{8} + 8\frac{1}{8} =$ ________

Name: ______________________________

Adding Mixed Numbers with Like Denominators

Focus on what you learned. Find the answers.

1. $5\frac{2}{8} + 6\frac{2}{8} =$ ________

2. $2\frac{1}{6} + 5\frac{4}{6} =$ ________

3. $10\frac{1}{4} + 12\frac{1}{4} =$ ________

4. $6\frac{1}{3} + 4\frac{2}{3} =$ ________

5. $7\frac{1}{5} + 6\frac{2}{5} =$ ________

6. $5\frac{3}{8} + 2\frac{1}{8} =$ ______

THINK & WRITE

Name: ______________________________

Adding Mixed Numbers with Like Denominators

Think about adding mixed numbers with like denominators. Write about what you learned.

1. What is a mixed number?

____

____

____

2. What is $4\frac{3}{5} + 3\frac{1}{5}$? How do you know?

____

____

____

____

3. Explain how to add mixed numbers with like denominators.

____

____

____

Name: ______________________________

Subtracting Mixed Numbers with Like Denominators

We know how to add mixed numbers with the same denominator.

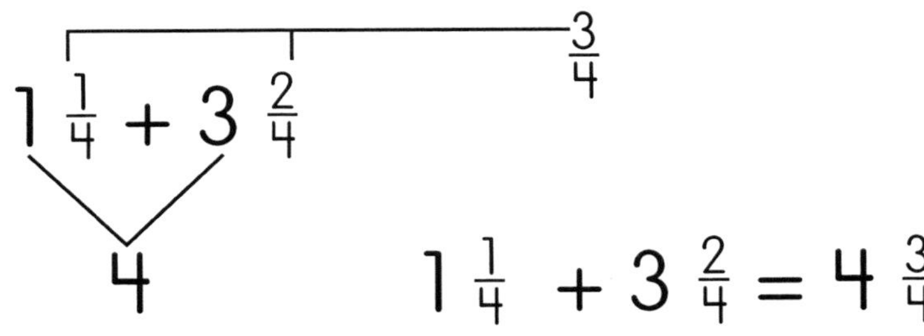

We can also subtract mixed numbers with the same denominator.

$$3\frac{4}{5} - 1\frac{1}{5}$$

We can break the mixed number into smaller parts: $3 - 1$ and $\frac{4}{5} - \frac{1}{5}$.

$$3 - 1 = 2$$

$$\frac{4}{5} - \frac{1}{5} = \frac{3}{5}$$

So, $3\frac{4}{5} - 1\frac{1}{5} = 2\frac{3}{5}$.

Name: ______________________________

Subtracting Mixed Numbers with Like Denominators

Work with your partner to solve these practice problems.

1. $5\frac{2}{3} - 2\frac{1}{3} =$ ________

2. $10\frac{3}{4} - 1\frac{1}{4} =$ ________

3. $12\frac{7}{8} - 8\frac{1}{8} =$ ________

4. $4\frac{1}{2} - 2\frac{1}{2} =$ ________

5. $6\frac{6}{9} - 3\frac{4}{9} =$ ________

6. $9\frac{6}{8} - 8\frac{3}{8} =$ ________

Name: ______________________________

Subtracting Mixed Numbers with Like Denominators

Focus on what you learned. Find the answers.

1. $4\frac{7}{8} - 2\frac{1}{8} =$ ________

2. $13\frac{2}{4} - 10\frac{1}{4} =$ ________

3. $9\frac{2}{8} - 3\frac{2}{8} =$ ________

4. $7\frac{6}{10} - 5\frac{5}{10} =$ ________

5. $10\frac{4}{5} - 3\frac{3}{5} =$ ________

6. $8\frac{4}{6} - 8\frac{3}{6} =$ ________

Name: ____________________

Subtracting Mixed Numbers with Like Denominators

Think about subtracting mixed numbers with like denominators. Write about what you learned.

1. Write an example of a mixed number. Explain the parts of the mixed number.

____

____

____

2. How is subtracting mixed numbers similar to adding mixed numbers?

____

____

____

____

3. One helpful hint for subtracting mixed numbers with like denominators is

____

____

____

Name: ______________________________

Multiplying a Fraction by a Whole Number

We know that multiplication can be represented as groups of objects times the number of objects in those groups.

$5 \times 2 = 10$

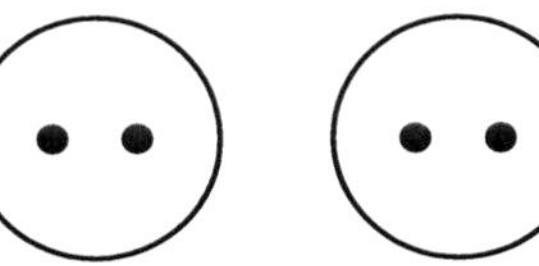

We can also multiply fractions by whole numbers using visual models to show groups of fractions.

For example, we can represent $4 \times \frac{1}{3}$ as 4 groups of $\frac{1}{3}$.

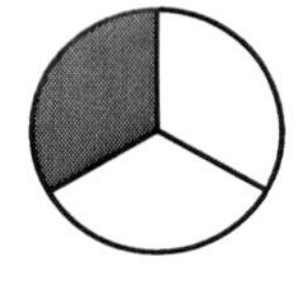
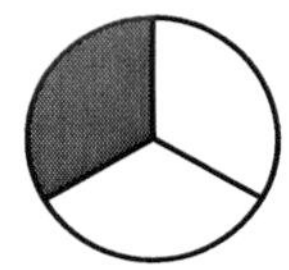
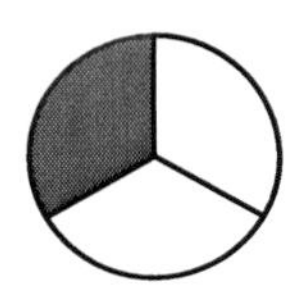
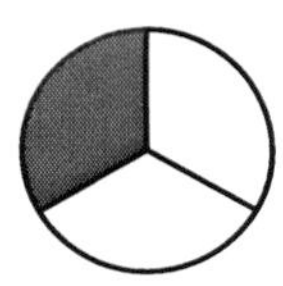

$$4 \times \frac{1}{3} = \frac{4}{1} \times \frac{1}{3} = \frac{4}{3}$$

Since the numerator is bigger than the denominator, this is an improper fraction. We can write it as a mixed number.

We can use division to change the improper fraction to a mixed number.

$$\frac{4}{3} = 3 \overline{)4} = 1\frac{1}{3}$$

$$\begin{array}{r} 1 \\ 3\overline{)4} \\ -3 \\ \hline 1 \end{array}$$

We show the remainder as a fraction. The remainder becomes the numerator and the divisor becomes the denominator.

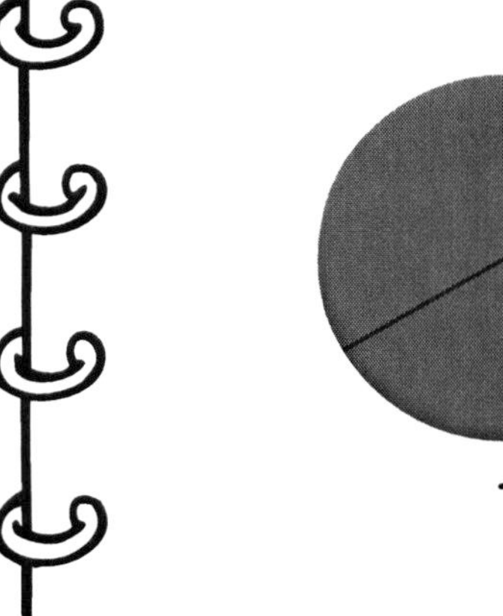
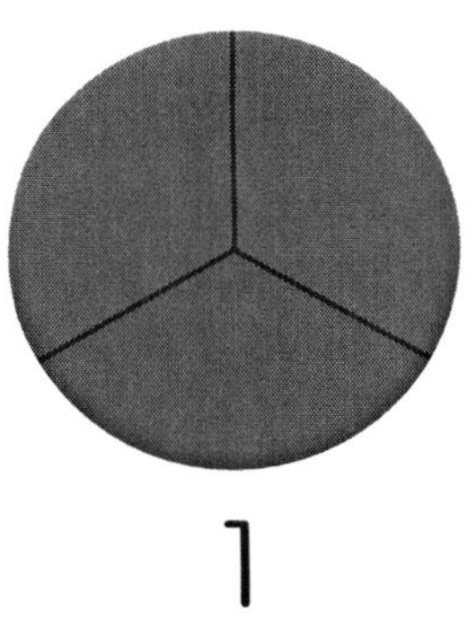

1

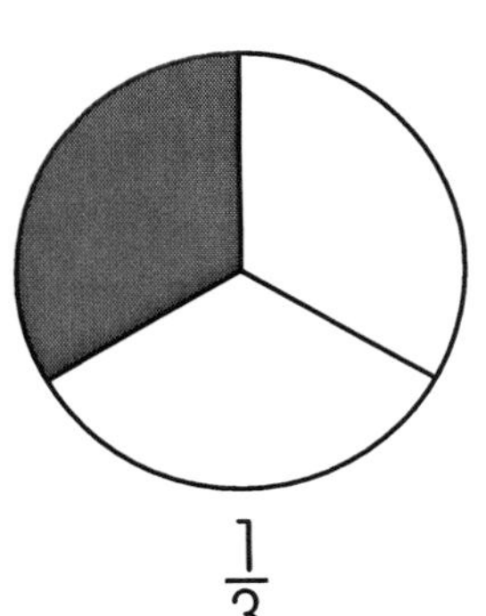

$\frac{1}{3}$

Name: ______________________________

Multiplying a Fraction by a Whole Number

Work with your partner to solve these practice problems.

Shade the visual models to solve each problem. Write improper fractions as mixed numbers.

1. $5 \times \frac{1}{2} =$ ________

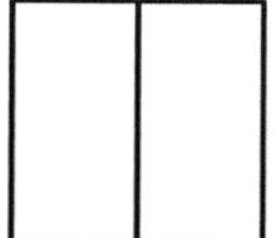
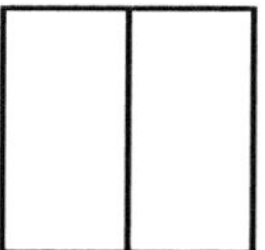
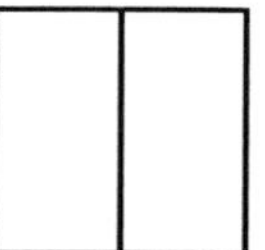
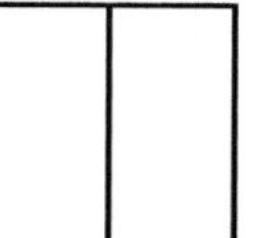
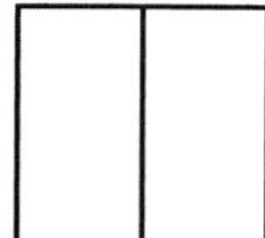

2. $2 \times \frac{1}{8} =$ ________

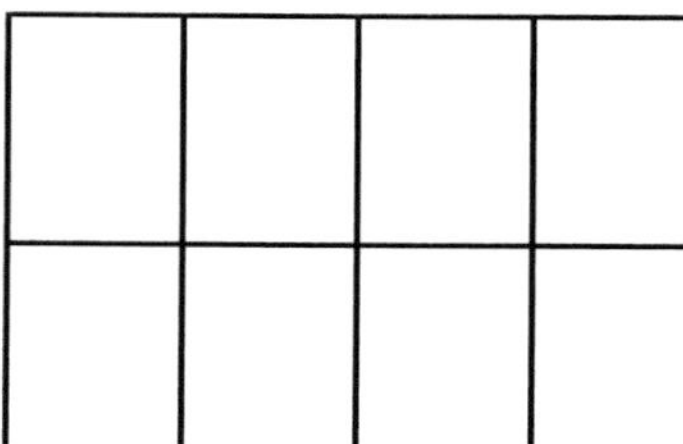

3. $6 \times \frac{1}{3} =$ ________

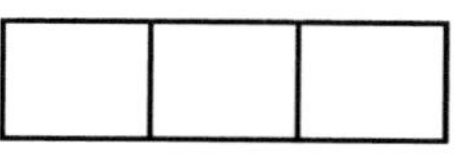
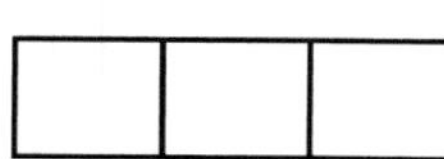

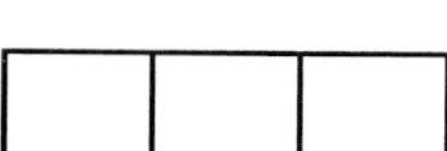

4. $3 \times \frac{3}{4} =$ ________

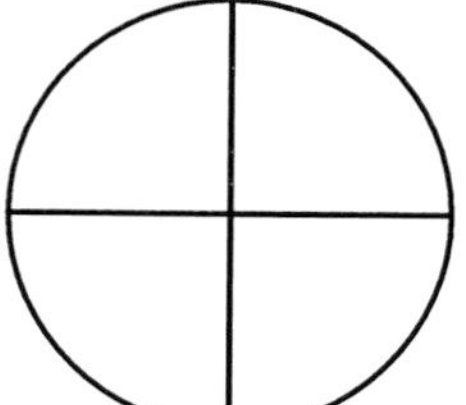
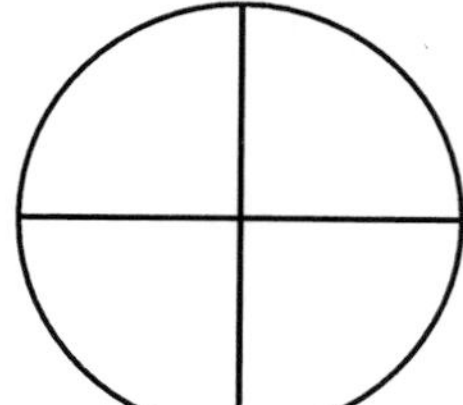
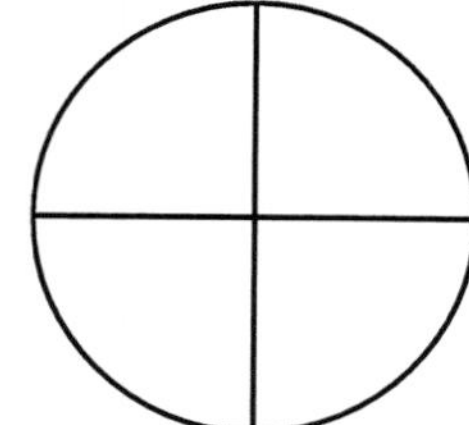

Name: ______________________________

Multiplying a Fraction by a Whole Number

Focus on what you learned. Find the answers.

Draw a visual model to solve each problem. Write improper fractions as mixed numbers.

1. $8 \times \frac{1}{3} =$ __________

2. $5 \times \frac{2}{4} =$ __________

3. $6 \times \frac{3}{5} =$ __________

4. $3 \times \frac{1}{8} =$ __________

Name: ______________________________

Multiplying a Fraction by a Whole Number

Think about multiplying fractions by whole numbers. Write about what you learned.

1. How do visual models help you multiply fractions by whole numbers?

____

____

____

____

2. What is an improper fraction?

____

____

____

3. One important thing to remember when multiplying a fraction by a whole number is

____

____

____

Name: ______________________________

Decimal Notation

The visual models below represent the fractions $\frac{4}{10}$ and $\frac{65}{100}$.

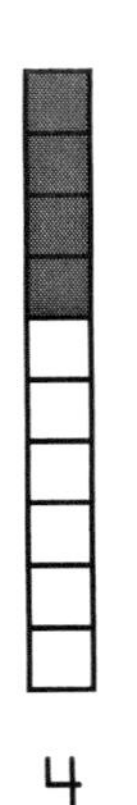

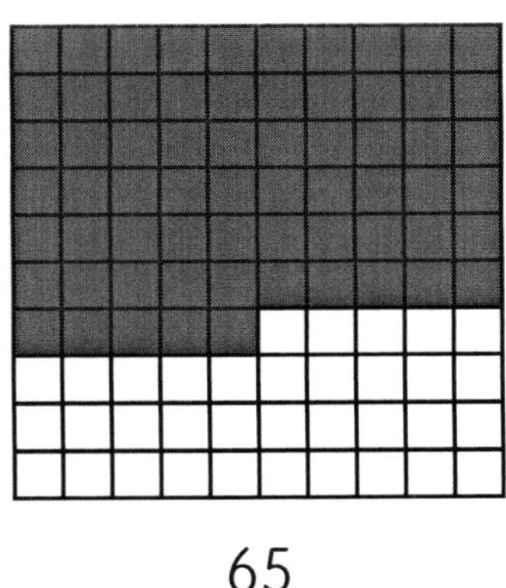

$\frac{4}{10}$ $\frac{65}{100}$

Fractions with denominators of 10 and 100 can also be written as decimals.

hundreds	tens	ones	.	tenths	hundredths

Decimals are less than 1 whole. They use place value places to the right of the decimal point.

$\frac{4}{10} = 0.4$ ← Like the fraction, this decimal is read as "four tenths."

$\frac{65}{100} = 0.65$ ← Like the fraction, this decimal is read as "sixty-five hundredths."

Name: ____________________

Decimal Notation

Work with your partner to solve these practice problems.

Write each fraction using decimal notation.

1. $\frac{5}{10} =$ ____________

2. $\frac{72}{100} =$ ____________

3. $\frac{17}{100} =$ ____________

4. $\frac{3}{10} =$ ____________

5. $\frac{89}{100} =$ ____________

6. $\frac{9}{10} =$ ____________

7. $\frac{4}{10} =$ ____________

8. $\frac{40}{100} =$ ____________

Name: ______________________________

Decimal Notation

Focus on what you learned. Find the answers.

Write each fraction using decimal notation.

1. $\frac{2}{10}$ = ______________

2. $\frac{27}{100}$ = ______________

3. $\frac{34}{100}$ = ______________

4. $\frac{1}{10}$ = ______________

5. $\frac{5}{100}$ = ______________

6. $\frac{8}{10}$ = ______________

7. $\frac{6}{10}$ = ______________

8. $\frac{61}{100}$ = ______________

Name: ______________________________

Decimal Notation

Think about decimal notation. Write about what you learned.

1. Why do you have to understand place value in order to use decimal notation?

____

____

____

____

2. How are fractions and decimals related?

____

____

____

3. I feel (confident/confused) about working with decimals because

____

____

____

Name: ______________________________

Comparing Decimals

We know how to compare two fractions by determining whether a fraction is greater than (>), less than (<), or equal to (=) another fraction.

$$\frac{1}{4} < \frac{1}{2}$$

But, how do we compare decimals?

We can rewrite each decimal as a fraction and then compare.

$$0.7 \;(?)\; 0.12$$

$$\frac{7}{10} \;(?)\; \frac{12}{100}$$

Let's convert
$\frac{7}{10}$ so it has
the same
denominator.

$$\frac{7}{10} \times \frac{10}{10} = \frac{70}{100}$$

$$\frac{70}{100} > \frac{12}{100}$$

$$0.7 > 0.12$$

We can also use a visual model to help us compare decimals.

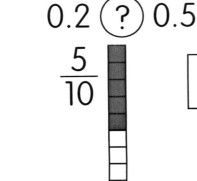

$$0.2 \;(?)\; 0.5$$

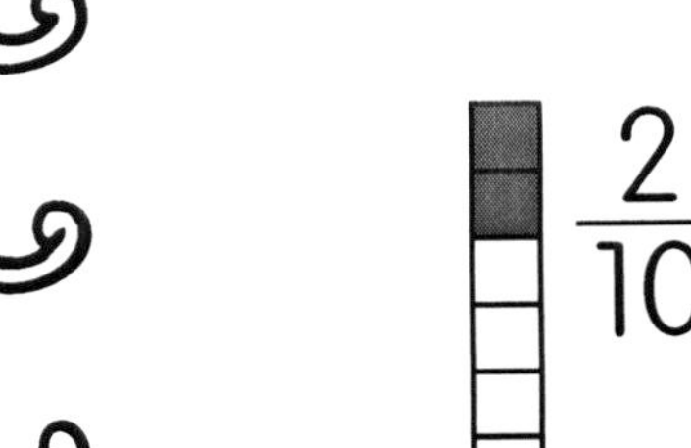

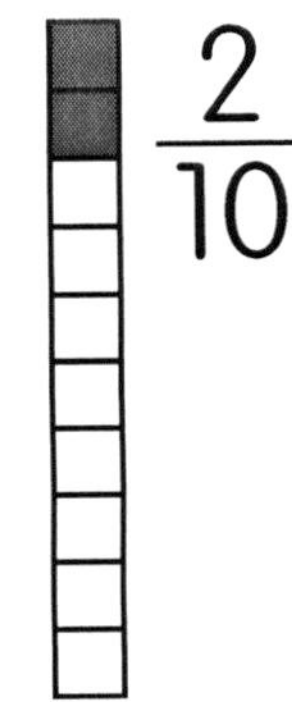

$\frac{2}{10}$ $\frac{5}{10}$

$$0.2 < 0.5$$

Name: ______________________

Comparing Decimals

Work with your partner to solve these practice problems.

Rewrite each decimal as a fraction. Then, compare the decimals using >, <, or =.

1. 0.25 ◯ 0.70

_______ _______

2. 0.6 ◯ 0.5

_______ _______

3. 0.65 ◯ 0.31

_______ _______

4. 0.41 ◯ 0.4

_______ _______

Shade the visual model for each decimal. Then, compare the decimals using >, <, or =.

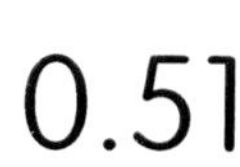

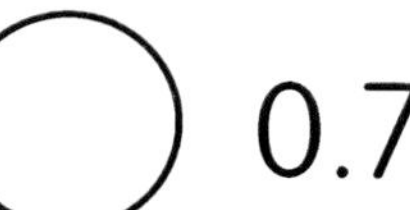

5. 0.51 ◯ 0.75

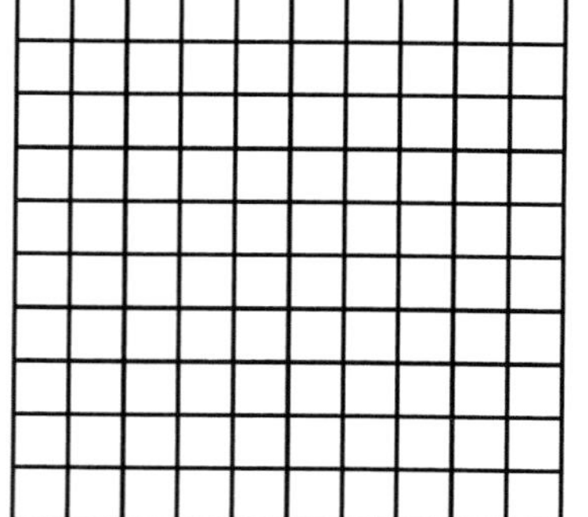

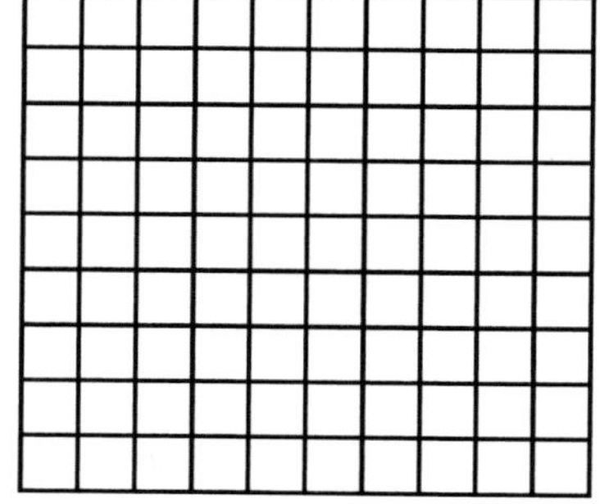

6. 0.6 ◯ 0.3

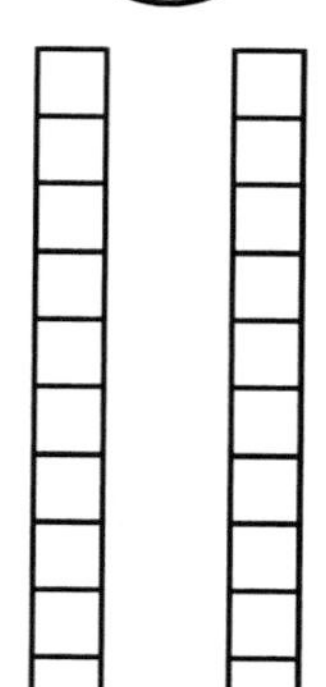

Name: ______________________________

Comparing Decimals

Focus on what you learned. Find the answers.

Rewrite each decimal as a fraction. Then, compare the decimals using >, <, or =.

1. 0.43 ◯ 0.4

   __________ __________

2. 0.3 ◯ 0.35

   __________ __________

3. 0.08 ◯ 0.8

   __________ __________

4. 0.75 ◯ 0.70

   __________ __________

Shade the visual model for each decimal. Then, compare the decimals using >, <, or =.

5. 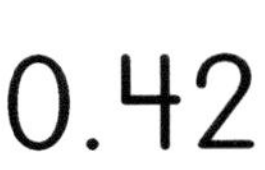 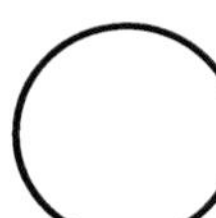 0.40

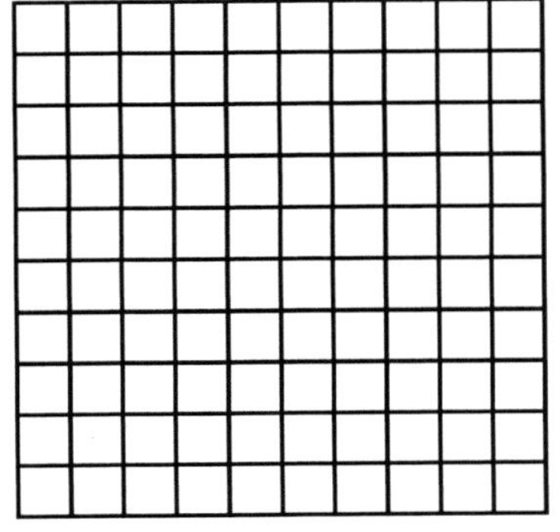

6. 0.4 ◯ 0.8

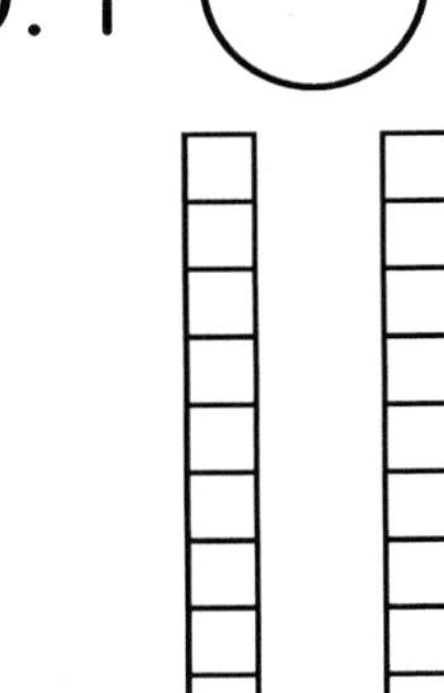

THINK & WRITE

Name: ______________________________

Comparing Decimals

Think about comparing decimals. Write about what you learned.

1. What strategy for comparing decimals works best for you? Explain.

2. Is the inequality true? How do you know?

$$0.3 < 0.35$$

3. Write about a situation in the real world in which you may have to compare decimals.

Name: ________________________________

Conversions

We can measure lengths using centimeters (cm), meters (m), and kilometers (km).

$$100 \text{ cm} = 1 \text{ m}$$

$$1{,}000 \text{ m} = 1 \text{ km}$$

We can use multiplication and division to convert measurements.

Sam draws a line that is 2 meters long. How many centimeters is the line?

$$2 \text{ m} \times 100 = 200 \text{ cm}$$

Rose walks 3,000 meters. How many kilometers does she walk?

$$3{,}000 \text{ m} \div 1{,}000 = 3 \text{ km}$$

Name: ______________________

Conversions

Work with your partner to solve these practice problems.

Convert the measurements.

1. 1,000 cm = ______ m
2. 5,000 m = ______ km
3. 12 m = ________ cm
4. 500 cm = ______ m
5. 4 km = ________ m
6. 10,000 m = _____ km

Name: ______________________________

Conversions

Focus on what you learned. Find the answers.

Convert the measurements.

1. 1,000 m = ______ km

2. 5,000 cm = ______ m

3. 16 m = __________ cm

4. 10 km = __________ m

5. Taylor rides her bike 7 kilometers. How many meters does she ride?

________ m

6. Bob cuts a piece of string that measures 500 centimeters. How many meters is the string?

________ m

Name: ______________________________

Conversions

Think about conversions. Write about what you learned.

1. How are multiplication and division related to converting measurements? Explain with an example.

____

____

____

____

2. How many meters are in 9 kilometers? How do you know?

____

____

____

____

3. When I think of conversions, I think ______________________________

____

____

____

Name: ______________________________

Line Plots

We can use a line plot to organize data. A line plot is a type of graph. It shows the frequency of data on a number line.

The data table to the right shows the fraction of an inch that different plants grew in a month.

Plant	Growth (in inches)
tomato	$\frac{1}{2}$
kale	$\frac{3}{4}$
cucumber	$\frac{1}{2}$
lettuce	$\frac{1}{4}$
corn	$\frac{1}{2}$

This data can be displayed on a line plot.

Plants' Growth

x = 1 plant

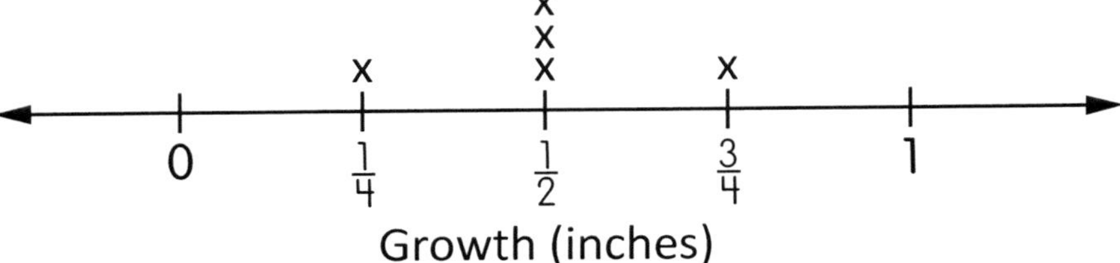

The line plot organizes the data to show that 1 plant grew $\frac{1}{4}$ in., 3 plants grew $\frac{1}{2}$ in., and 1 plant grew $\frac{3}{4}$ in.

Name: ____________________________________

Line Plots

Work with your partner to solve these practice problems.

1. Complete the line plot to show the data on the table. Use x to represent 1 student.

Student	Hours Spent on Homework
Tim	$\frac{1}{2}$
May	$\frac{3}{4}$
Lynn	$\frac{3}{4}$
Finn	$\frac{1}{4}$
Tatum	1
Beckett	$\frac{3}{4}$

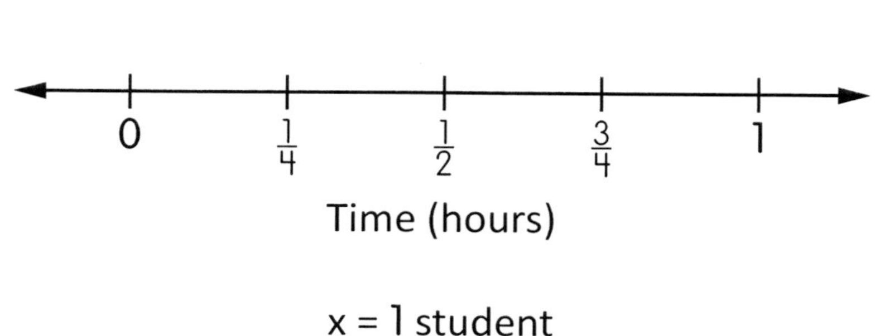

2. How many students spent more than $\frac{1}{2}$ of an hour on homework? __________

3. How long did most students spend on homework? __________

4. How many students spent less than $\frac{3}{4}$ of an hour on homework? __________

Name: ____________________________

Line Plots

Focus on what you learned. Find the answers.

Use the line plot to answer the questions.

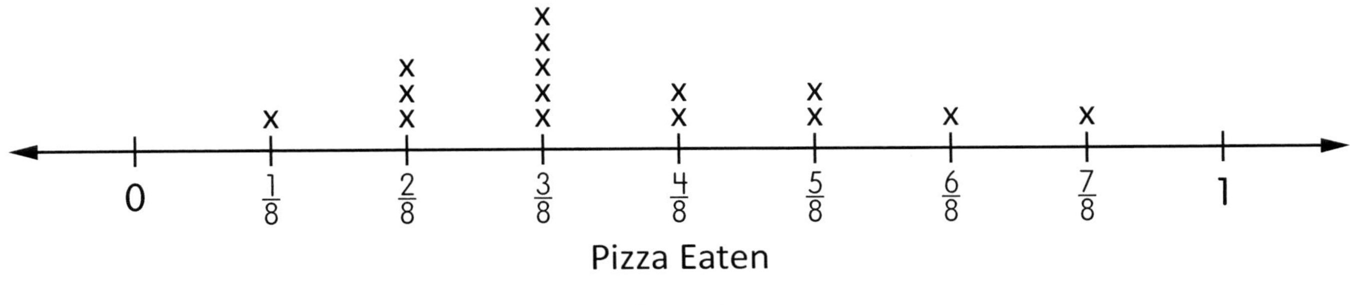

1. How many students ate pizza? ____________

2. How many students ate more than $\frac{3}{8}$ of a pizza? ____________

3. How many students ate less than $\frac{3}{8}$ of a pizza? ____________

4. What is the difference between the number of students who ate $\frac{3}{8}$ of a pizza and $\frac{1}{8}$ of a pizza?

____

THINK & WRITE

Name: ______________________________

Line Plots

Think about line plots. Write about what you learned.

1. What is the purpose of a line plot?

____

____

____

____

2. List three types of data you could organize on a line plot.

____

____

____

____

3. I (like/dislike) line plots because ______________________________

____

____

____

Name: ______________________________

Lines, Segments, and Rays

A **line** is a straight path that continues forever in both directions.

A **line segment** is part of a line. It has two endpoints.

A **ray** is part of a line. It has one endpoint and the other side continues in that direction forever.

Name: ______________________________

Lines, Segments, and Rays

Work with your partner to solve these practice problems.

Write *line*, *line segment*, or *ray* to identify each picture.

1. ______________________________

2. ______________________________

3. ______________________________

4. 1 2 3 4 5

____

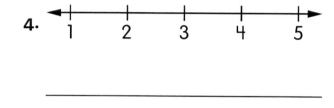

5. Draw a shape that is formed by 4 line segments.

Name: ______________________________

Lines, Segments, and Rays

Focus on what you learned. Find the answers.

1. Draw a line segment.

2. Draw a ray.

3. Draw a line.

4. Draw a shape that is made from 3 line segments.

Name: ______________________________

Lines, Segments, and Rays

Think about lines, segments, and rays. Write about what you learned.

1. What is a ray? How is it different from a line?

____

____

____

2. What is a line segment? How is it different from a line?

____

____

____

3. Write a short poem or joke about a line, a line segment, or a ray.

____

____

____

____

____

Name: ______________________________

Angles

Angles are formed where two line segments meet.

Some line segments meet at a 90 degree angle. This is called a **right angle**.

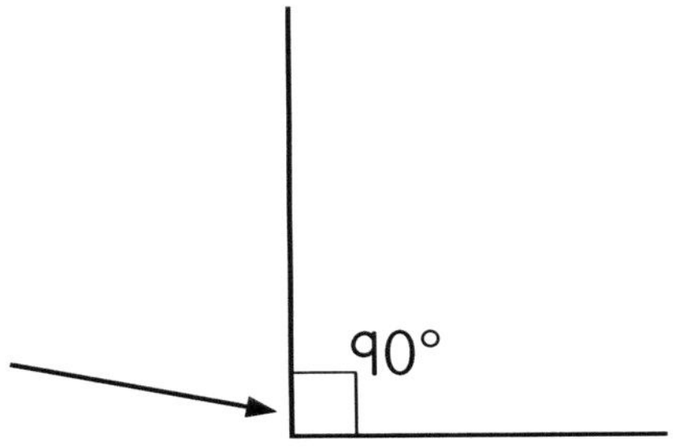

90°

An angle that is greater than 90 degrees is called an **obtuse angle**.

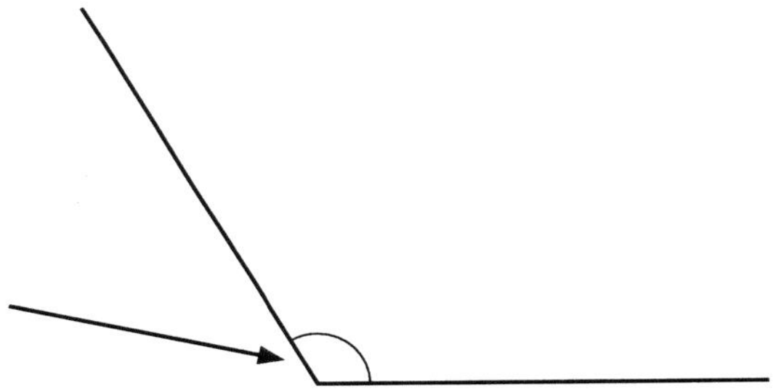

An angle that is less than 90 degrees is called an **acute angle**.

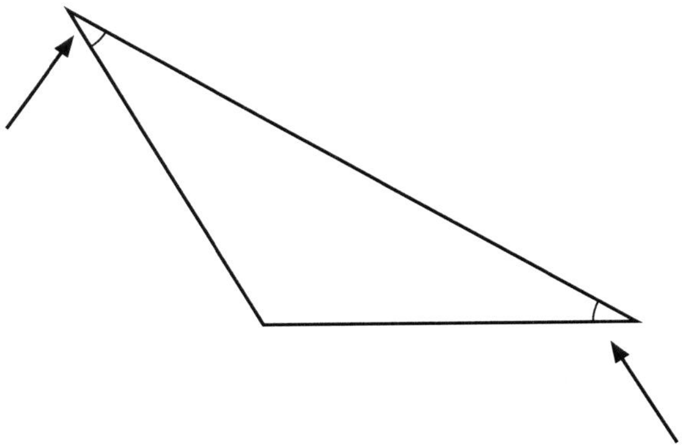

Name: ______________________________

Angles

Work with your partner to solve these practice problems.

Label each angle as *right*, *acute*, or *obtuse*.

1. 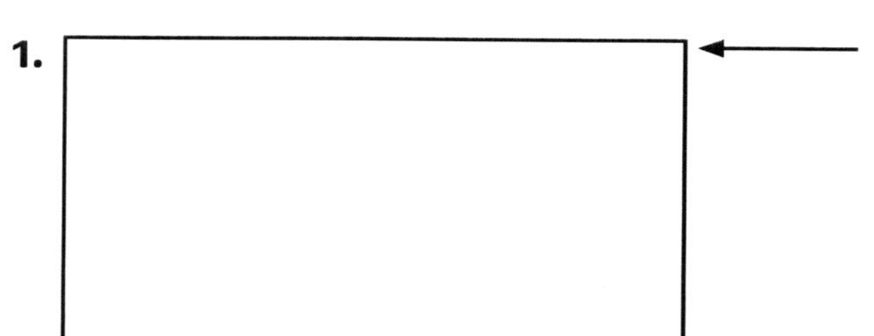

____

2. 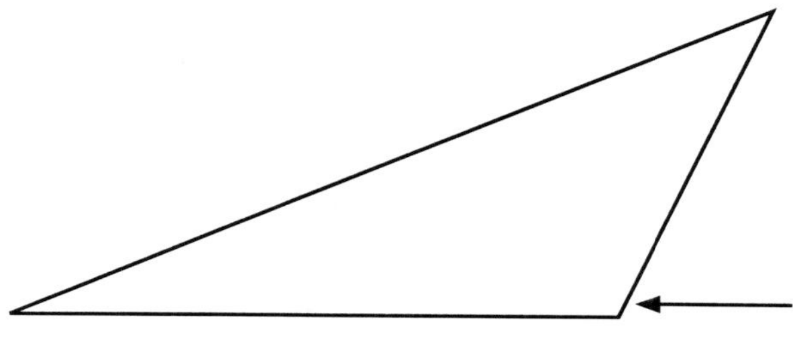

____

3. 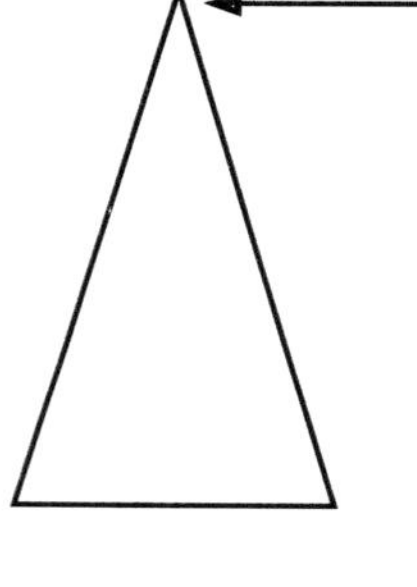

____

4. 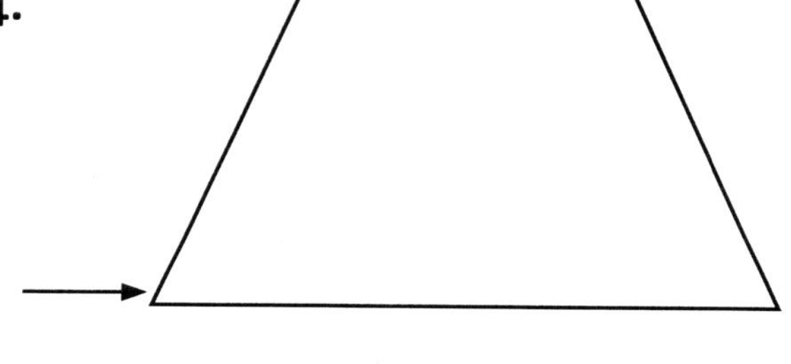

____

5. Label each angle in the figure.

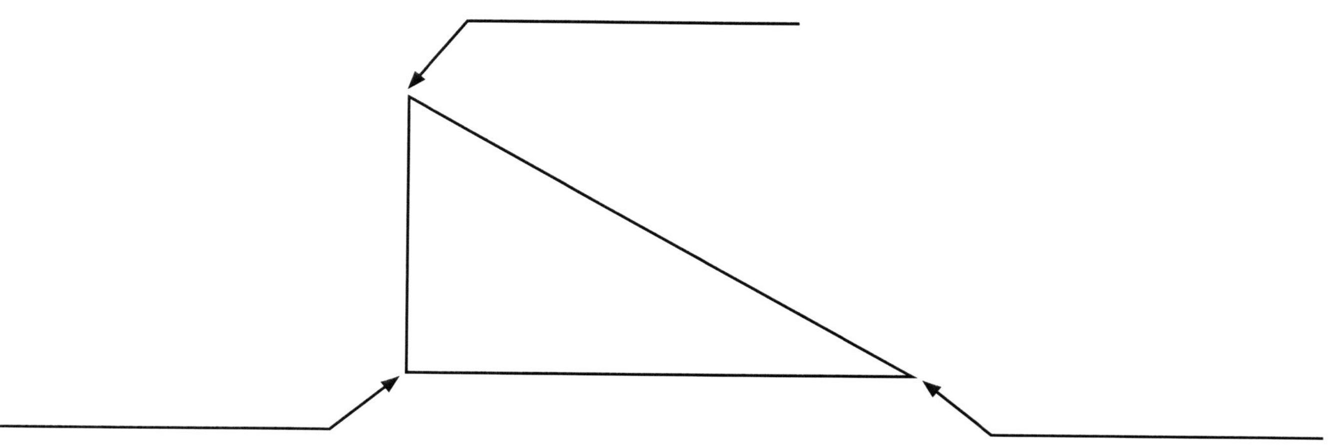

Name: ____________________________________

Angles

Focus on what you learned. Find the answers.

Label each angle as *right*, *acute*, or *obtuse*.

1.

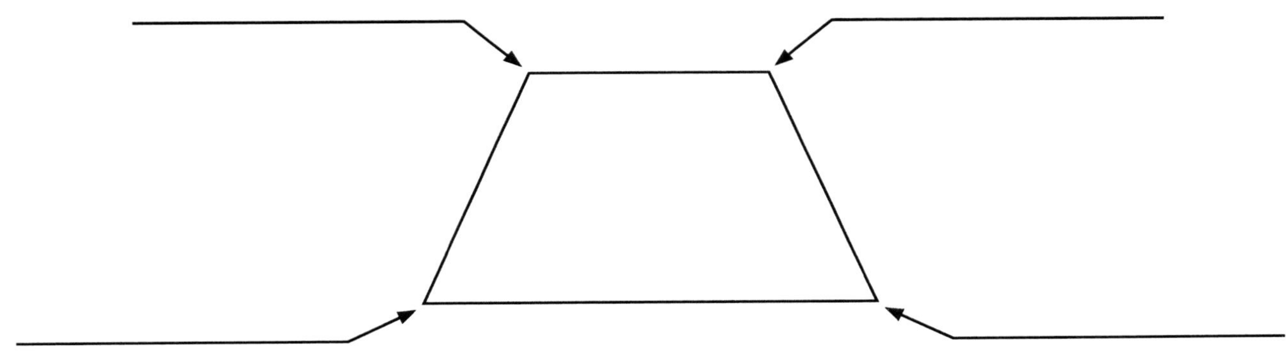

2.

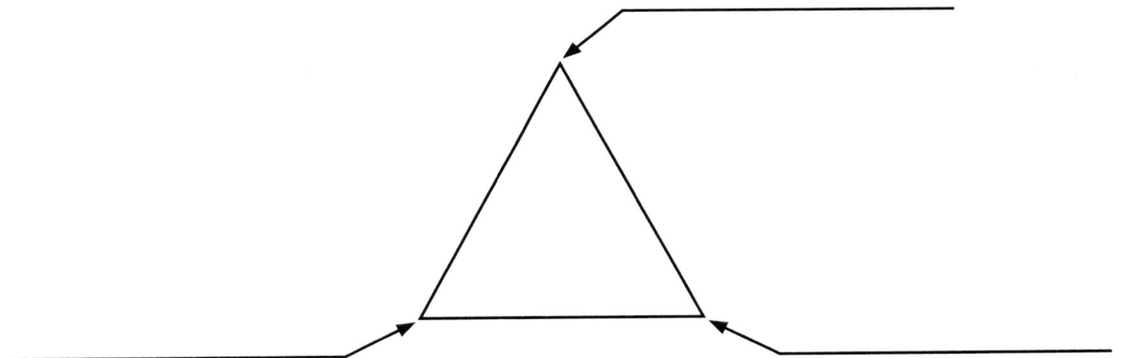

3. Draw a figure with at least one right angle. Label each angle.

Name: ______________________________

Angles

Think about angles. Write about what you learned.

1. Is the angle marked below right, acute, or obtuse? How do you know?

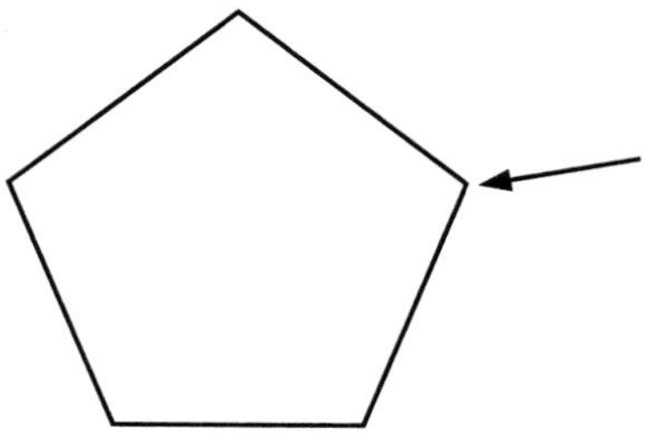

____

____

____

2. Do figures have only one type of angle or more than one type? Explain with examples.

____

____

____

____

3. What is your favorite type of angle? Why?

____

____

Name: ______________________________

Classifying 2-D Figures

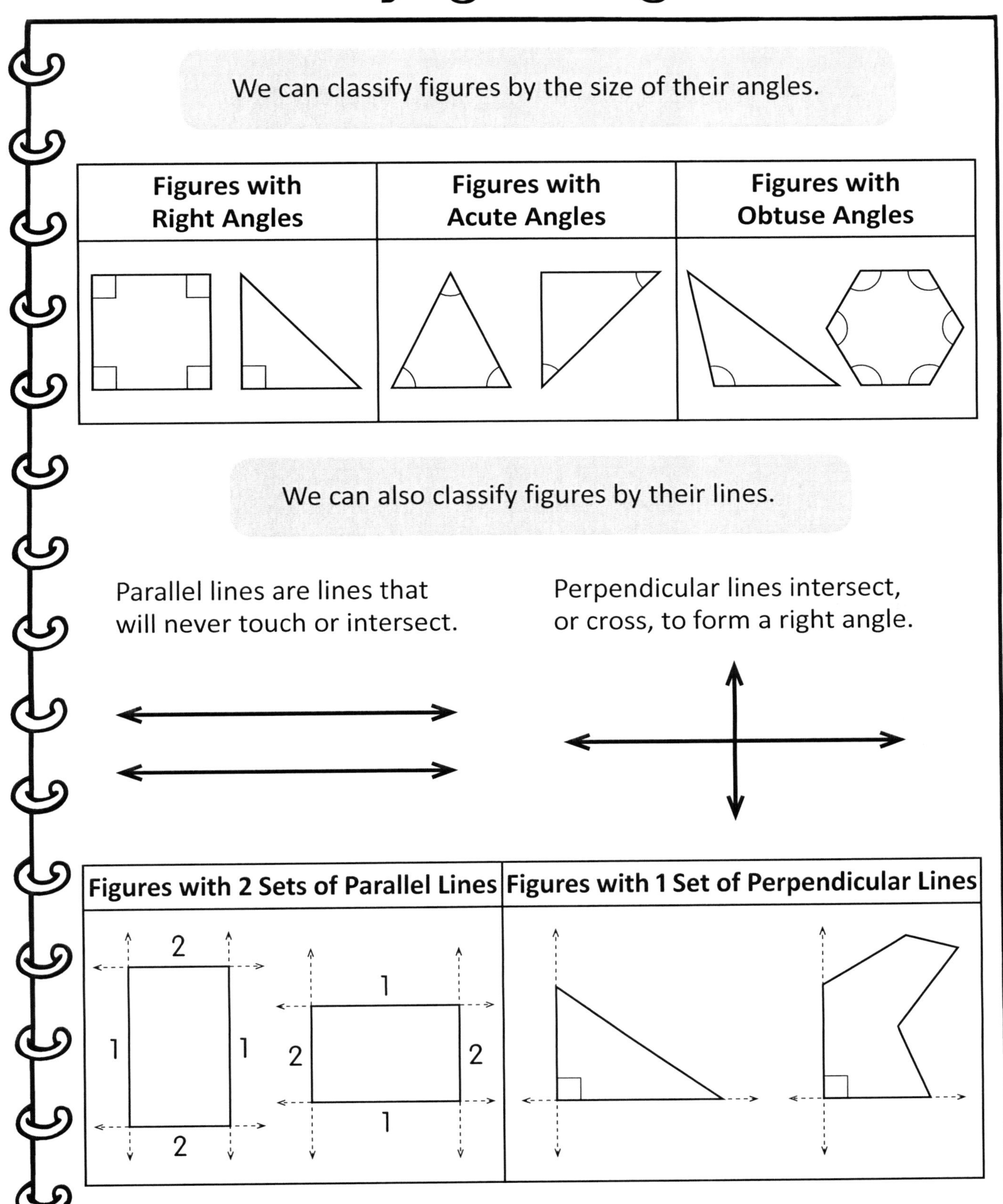
We can classify figures by the size of their angles.
Figures with Right Angles
Figures with Acute Angles
Figures with Obtuse Angles
We can also classify figures by their lines.
Parallel lines are lines that will never touch or intersect.
Perpendicular lines intersect, or cross, to form a right angle.
Figures with 2 Sets of Parallel Lines
Figures with 1 Set of Perpendicular Lines
2
1
1
2
1
2
2
1

Name: ______________________________

Classifying 2-D Figures

Work with your partner to solve these practice problems.

Write *parallel* or *perpendicular* to classify the lines the arrows are pointing to in each figure.

1.

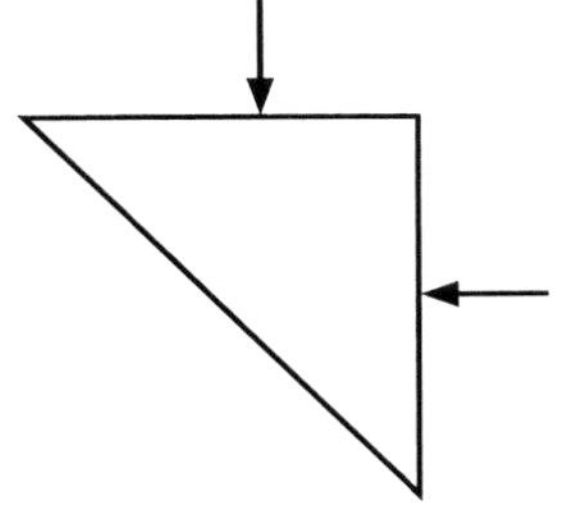

____

2.

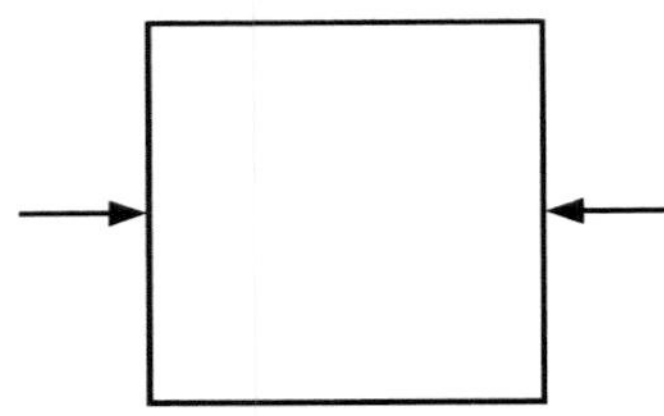

____

3.

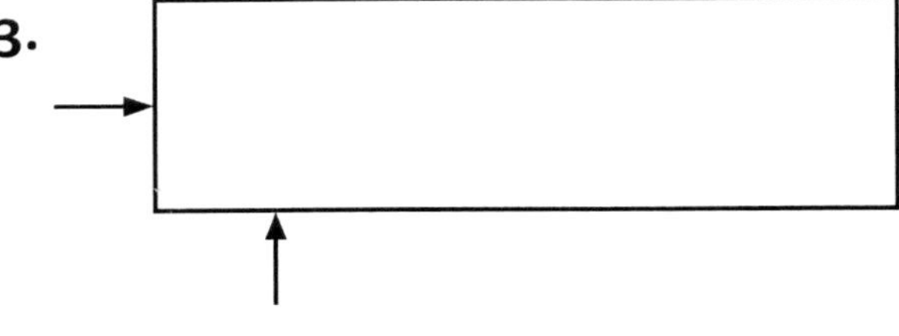

____

4.

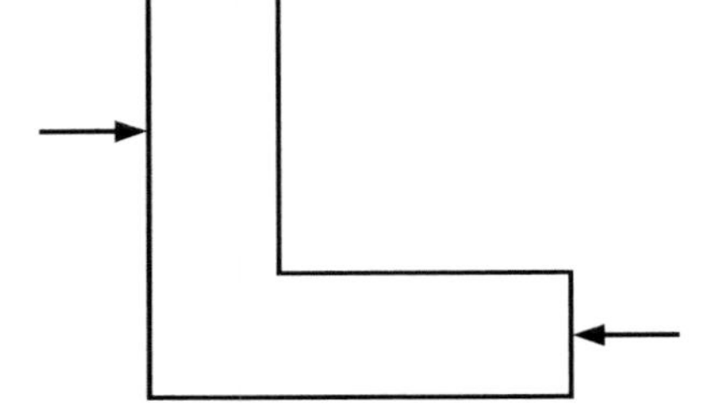

____

Write *right*, *acute*, or *obtuse* to tell about each angle.

5.

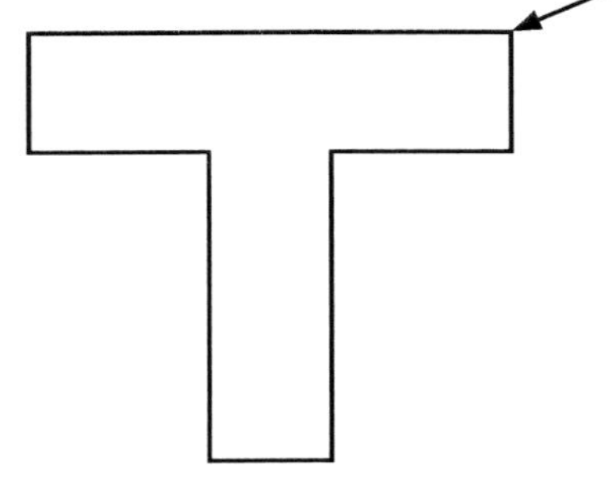

____

6.

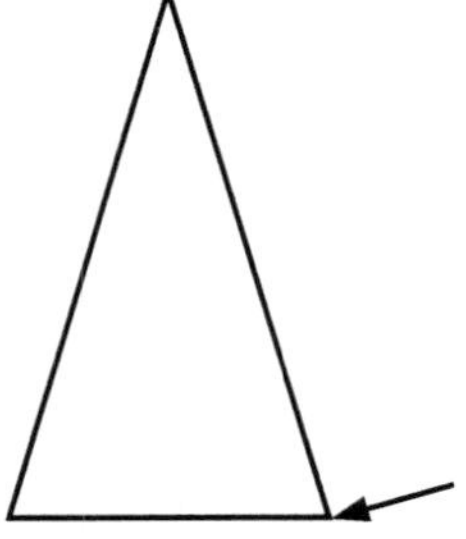

____

Name: ______________________________

Classifying 2-D Figures

Focus on what you learned. Find the answers.

Draw at least **two** figures for each category on the chart.

Figures with 2 Sets of Parallel Lines	Figures with No Parallel Lines	Figures with 1 Set of Perpendicular Lines
Figures with More Than 1 Right Angle	**Figures with at Least 1 Acute Angle**	**Figures with at Least 1 Obtuse Angle**

Name: ______________________________

Classifying 2-D Figures

Think about classifying 2-D figures. Write about what you learned.

1. What are parallel and perpendicular lines?

____

____

____

2. Is it possible for a figure to be classified into more than one category? Why, or why not?

____

____

____

____

3. To help me remember how to classify 2-D figures, I will ______________

____

____

____

Name: ______________________________

Lines of Symmetry

A line of symmetry is a line that divides a figure into matching parts.

Imagine that we fold a figure in half. Both halves must be exactly the same to have symmetry.

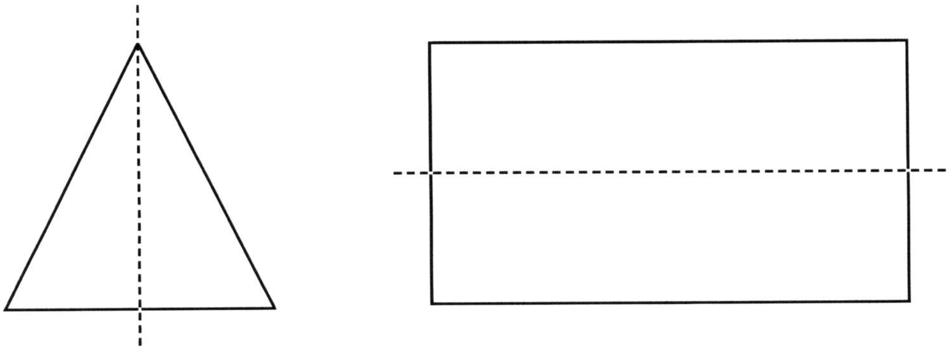

Some figures have more than one line of symmetry.

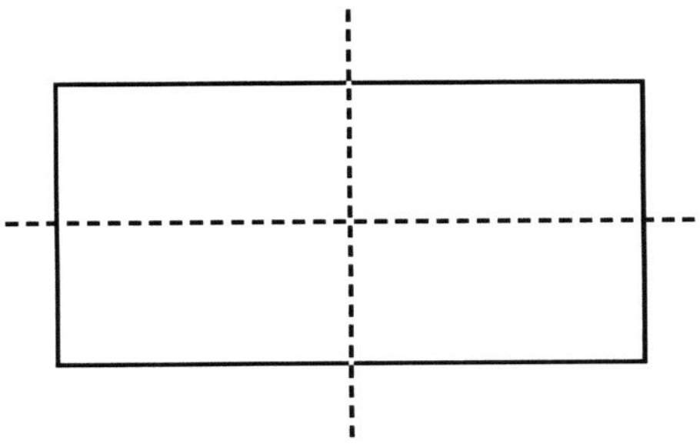

Some figures do not have any lines of symmetry.

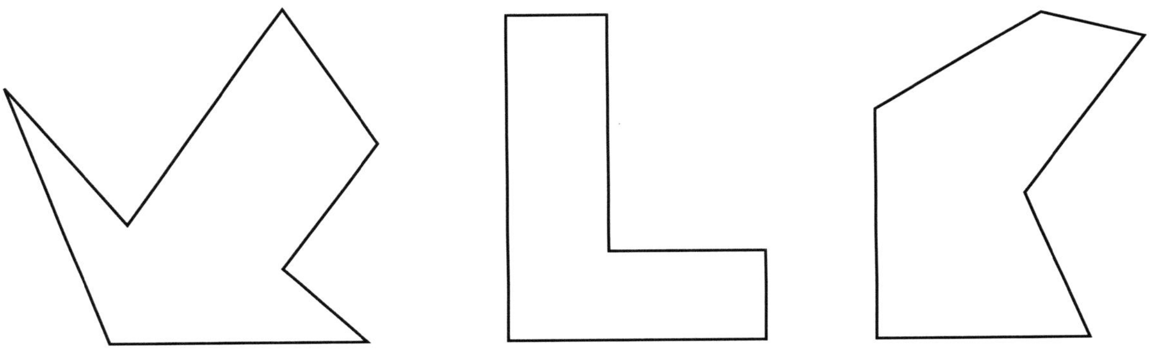

Name: ______________________________

Lines of Symmetry

Work with your partner to solve these practice problems.

Write *yes* or *no* to tell whether the dashed line is a line of symmetry.

1.

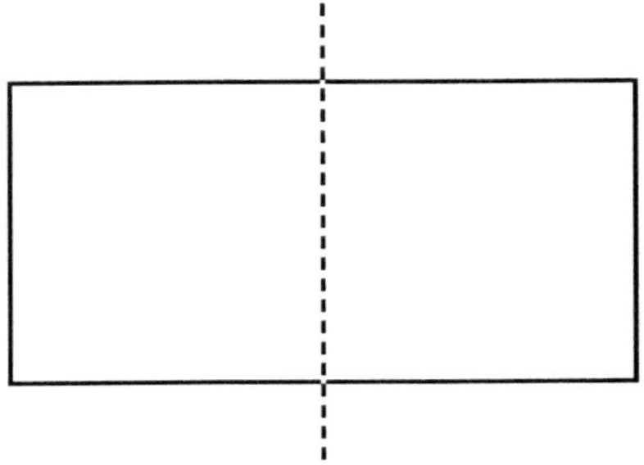

____

2.

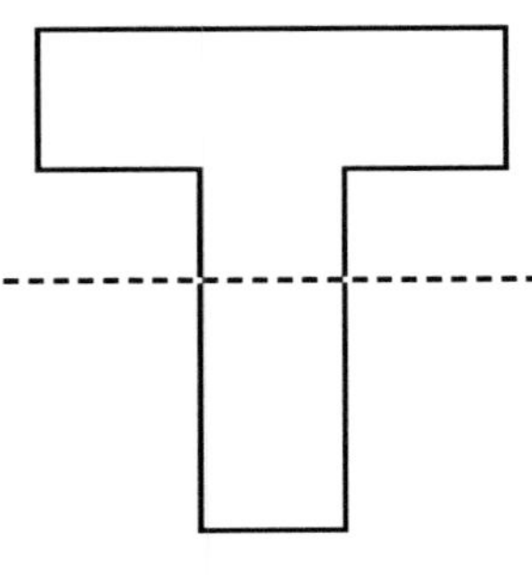

____

3.

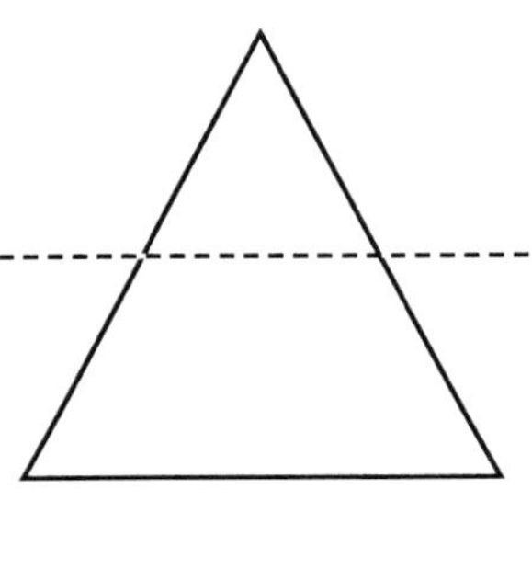

____

4.

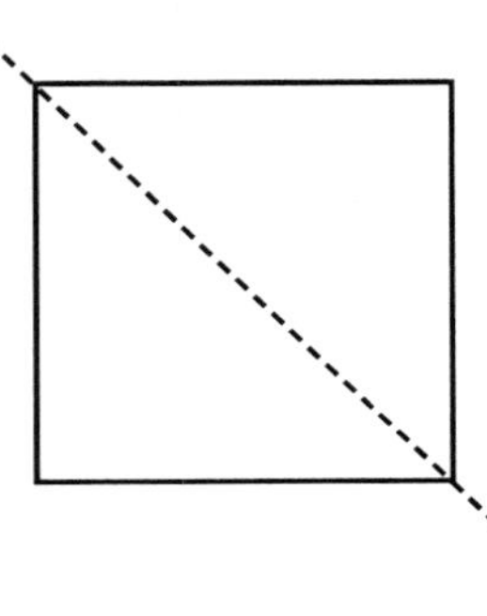

____

Draw a line of symmetry on each figure.

5.

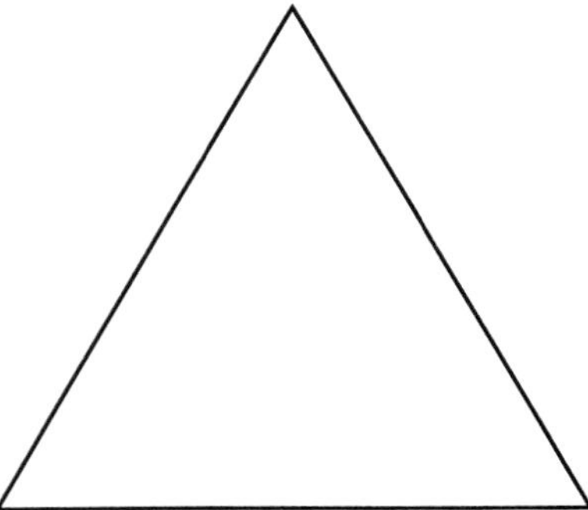

6.

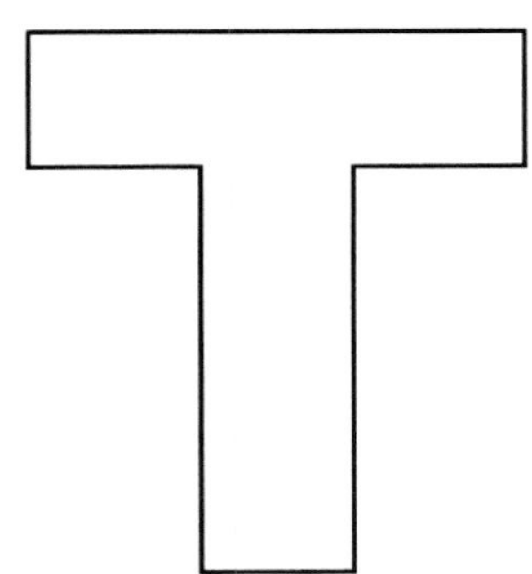

Name: ______________________________

Lines of Symmetry

Focus on what you learned. Find the answers.

Draw a line of symmetry for each figure.

1. 

2. 

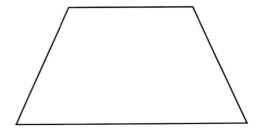

3. 

4. 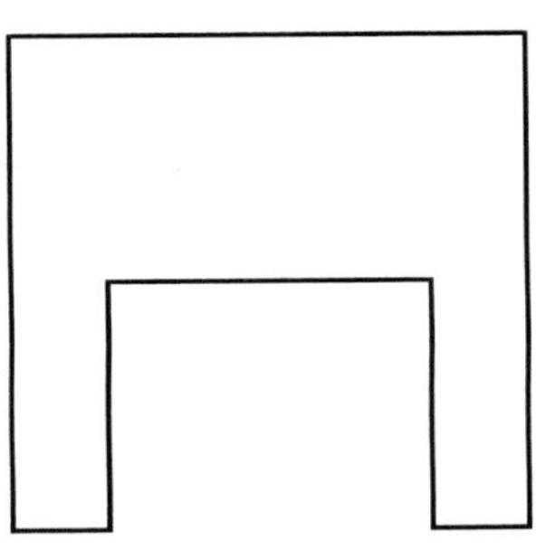

5. 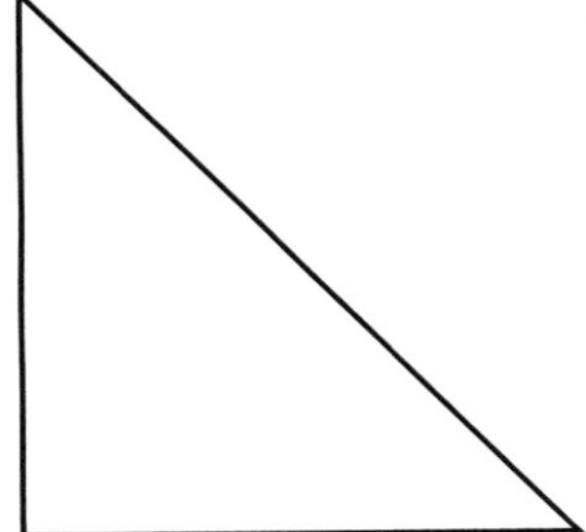

6. 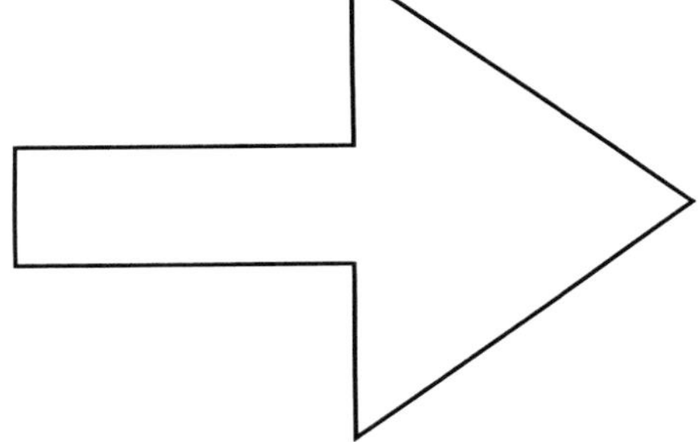

Name: ____________________________

Lines of Symmetry

Think about lines of symmetry. Write about what you learned.

1. What is a line of symmetry?

____

____

____

2. Does the figure below have a line of symmetry? How do you know?

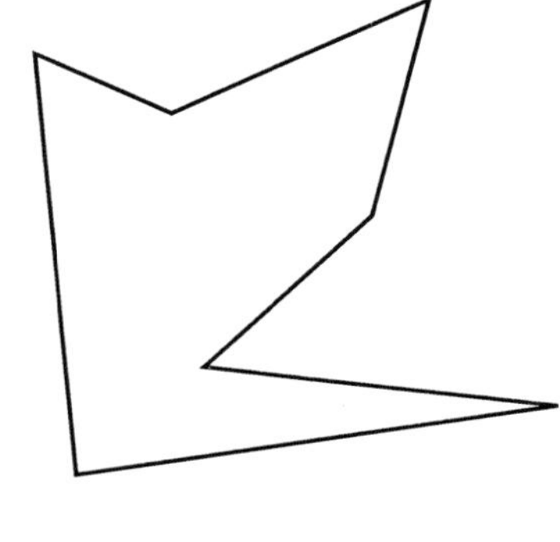

____

____

____

____

3. When I think of symmetry, I think ____________________________

____

____

READ & LEARN

Name: ____________________________________

Word Problems: Multi-Step

We know how to solve word problems using addition, subtraction, multiplication, and division.

Josh has 926 baseball cards. Suzy has 382 fewer cards than Josh. How many baseball cards does Suzy have?

$926 - 382 = 544$ Suzy has 544 baseball cards.

Some word problems have multiple steps to solve them. To solve these problems, we often have to use two or more operations.

Josue bakes 12 cupcakes for a party. Peter bakes 18 cupcakes. If there are 6 people at the party, how many cupcakes will each person get?

Step 1: $12 + 18 = 30$

Step 2: $30 \div 6 = 5$

Each person will get 5 cupcakes.

Name: ______________________________

Word Problems: Multi-Step

Work with your partner to solve these practice problems. Write your answers in complete sentences.

1. Sona reads 25 pages every Monday, 15 pages every Tuesday, and 32 pages every Wednesday. If she continues to read the same amounts every Monday, Tuesday, and Wednesday, how many pages will she read after 4 weeks?

Step 1:	**Step 2:**
Answer:	

2. Mr. Lee orders 15 pizzas for some fourth-grade students. Each pizza has 8 slices. How many students can Mr. Lee feed if each student gets 3 slices of pizza?

Step 1:	**Step 2:**
Answer:	

Name: ________________________________

Word Problems: Multi-Step

Focus on what you learned. Find the answers. Write your answers in complete sentences.

1. The fourth-graders from Tate School are going on a field trip. Class A has 25 students, class B has 32 students, and class C has 35 students. If the students are divided evenly on 2 buses, how many students will be on each bus?

Step 1:	**Step 2:**
Answer:	

2. Benny buys a pack of stickers. There are 5 sheets with 26 stickers on each sheet. If he divides the stickers among 10 friends, how many stickers will each friend get?

Step 1:	**Step 2:**
Answer:	

Name: ______________________________

Word Problems: Multi-Step

Think about solving multistep word problems. Write about what you learned.

1. What is a multistep word problem?

____

____

____

2. Write your own multistep word problem. Then solve it in the space below.

____

____

____

____

Name: ____________________________

Word Problems: Fractions

We know how to multiply, add, and subtract fractions.

$3 \times \frac{1}{2} = ?$ 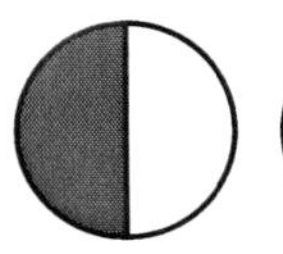 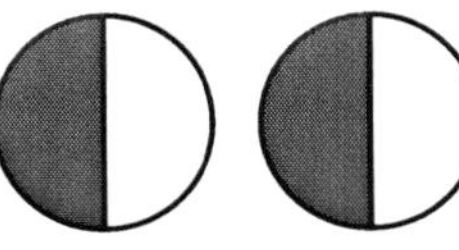 $3 \times \frac{1}{2} = \frac{3}{2} = 1\frac{1}{2}$

$\frac{1}{4} + \frac{1}{4} = ?$ 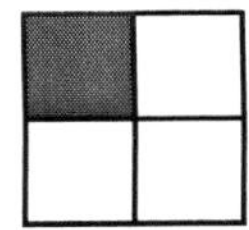 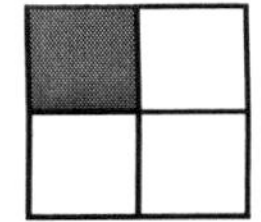 $\frac{1}{4} + \frac{1}{4} = \frac{2}{4} = \frac{1}{2}$

We can use what we know about fractions to solve word problems involving fractions.

Maya uses $\frac{2}{3}$ cup of flour for each batch of muffins. How much flour will she use if she bakes 3 batches of muffins?

$$\frac{2}{3} \times 3 = \frac{2}{3} \times \frac{3}{1} = \frac{6}{3} = 2$$

Maya will use 2 cups of flour.

You and 2 friends each have $\frac{1}{4}$ of a granola bar. How much do you and your friends have in all?

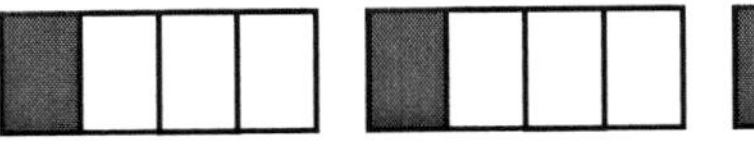

$$\frac{1}{4} + \frac{1}{4} + \frac{1}{4} \text{ or } 3 \times \frac{1}{4} = \frac{3}{4}$$

You and your friends have $\frac{3}{4}$ of a granola bar in all.

Name: ______________________________

Word Problems: Fractions

Work with your partner to solve these practice problems. Write your answers in complete sentences. Change improper fractions to mixed numbers.

1. You run $\frac{1}{3}$ mile every day. How far do you run in a week?

Visual Model:	**Equation:**
Solution:	

2. You read for $\frac{3}{4}$ of an hour every day. How much time do you spend reading after 5 days?

Visual Model:	**Equation:**
Solution:	

Name: ____________________

Word Problems: Fractions

Focus on what you learned. Find the answers. Write your answers in complete sentences. Change improper fractions to mixed numbers.

1. Matt has $\frac{7}{10}$ of a pizza. He shares $\frac{3}{10}$ with his friend. How much pizza does Matt have left?

Visual Model:	**Equation:**
Solution:	

2. At a party, each person will drink $\frac{3}{5}$ of a liter of punch. How many liters will 4 people drink?

Visual Model:	**Equation:**
Solution:	

Name: ________________________________

THINK & WRITE

Word Problems: Fractions

Think about solving word problems with fractions. Write about what you learned.

1. How do visual models help you solve word problems with fractions?

____

____

____

2. Read the problem below. Between what two whole numbers does the answer fall on a number line? How do you know? Draw a number line in the blank space below.

Four friends each have $\frac{4}{6}$ of a bag of popcorn. How much did they eat all together?

____

____

____

____

READ & LEARN

Name: ____________________

Word Problems: Measurement & Money

We can use what we know about the four operations to solve word problems involving measurement.

May cuts 6 pieces of string that each measure 6 inches. How many feet of string does she cut?

$6 \times 6 = 36$ inches

$36 \div 12 = ?$ or $? \times 12 = 36$

$36 \div 12 = \textcircled{3}$ $\textcircled{3} \times 12 = 36$

May cut 3 feet of string.

Greg spends $5.81 on a sandwich and $1.25 on a bottle of water. How much money does he spend in all?

$$\begin{array}{r} \overset{1}{}\\ \$5.81 \\ +\$1.25 \\ \hline \$7.06 \end{array}$$

Greg spends $7.06 in all.

Name: ______________________________

Word Problems: Measurement & Money

Work with your partner to solve these practice problems.

1. There are 10 bottles of water in a case. Each bottle has 16 ounces. How many ounces are in the whole case?

2. Evan weighs 65 lbs. and Rashid weighs 42 lbs. How much do they weigh in all?

3. Shane has $20. He spends $11.05 at the pet store. How much money does he have left?

4. Tess measures a piece of rope that is 500 centimeters. How many meters is the rope?

FOCUS & FIND

Name: ________________________________

Word Problems: Measurement & Money

Focus on what you learned. Find the answers.

1. Michael rides his bike 2 miles each day. How many miles does he ride in 2 weeks?

2. You buy five 1-lb. bags of candy. How many ounces of candy do you buy?

3. Mom drives 5 kilometers to work. How many meters does she drive?

4. You have $40 to buy a new backpack and lunch box. The backpack costs $25.48 with tax. The lunch box costs $14.25 with tax. Do you have enough money to buy both items? How much money, if any, will you have left?

THINK & WRITE

Name: ______________________________

Word Problems: Measurement & Money

Think about solving measurement word problems. Write about what you learned.

1. What strategy works best for you to solve measurement word problems?

____

____

____

2. Write your own word problem using measurement. Then, solve your problem in the space below.

____

____

____

____

Answer Key

Page 6

1. 1, 2, 3, 6
2. 1, 2, 4, 5, 10, 20
3. 1, 3, 5, 15
4. 1, 2, 4, 8, 16

Page 7

1. 1, 2, 3, 6, 9, 18
2. 1, 2, 4, 8
3. 1, 2, 7, 14

Page 8

1. Factors are the numbers that are multiplied together to get a given product.
2. The factors of 30 are 1, 2, 3, 5, 6, 10, 15, and 30. I know this because 1 × 30 = 30, 2 × 15 = 30, 3 × 10 = 30, and 5 × 6 = 30.
3. Answers will vary.

Page 10

1. 1 × 11= 11; prime
2. 1 × 12 = 12, 2 × 6 = 12, 3 × 4 = 12; composite
3. 1 × 21 = 21, 3 × 7 = 21; composite
4. 1 × 29 = 29; prime

Page 11

1. 1, 3, 9; composite
2. 1, 2, 7, 14; composite
3. 1, 17; prime
4. 1, 2, 4, 8, 16; composite
5. 1, 2, 5, 10; composite
6. 1, 13; prime
7. Answers will vary.
8. Answers will vary.

Page 12

1. A prime number has only 1 and itself as factors. A composite number has factors other than 1 and itself.
2. 15 is a composite number because it has more than the factors 1 and 15. 3 and 5 are also factors of 15.
3. Answers will vary.

Page 14

1. 19, 23
2. 24, 29
3. 32, 64; Rule: Multiply by 2
4. 13, 16; Rule: Add 3

Page 15

1. 12, 15; Rule: Add 3
2. 52, 62; Rule: Add 10
3. 42, 49; Rule: Add 7
4. 13, 11; Rule: Subtract 2

Page 16

1. They always follow a certain rule.
2. The rule for the pattern is *multiply by 3*. I know this because 1 × 3 = 3, 3 × 3 = 9, 9 × 3 = 27 and so on.
3. Answers will vary.

Page 18

1. 300
2. 1,540

Page 19

1. 310
2. 560
3. 600
4. 1,200
5. 6,000
6. 1,000

Page 20

1. A number line can help you visually see where a number falls and whether it is closer to one number or another.
2. 2,350; I know this because 2,345 is the midpoint between 2,340 and 2,350. When a number is in the exact middle, you round up.
3. Answers will vary.

Page 22

1. <
2. >
3. >
4. =
5. <
6. >
7. <
8. <

Page 23

1. <
2. >
3. <
4. >
5. Answers will vary. Accept 1,781 or lower.
6. Answers will vary. Accept 428 or higher.
7. 9,812
8. Answers will vary. Accept 520 or lower.

Page 24

1. When comparing two numbers, > means greater than, < means less than, and = means that two numbers are equal to each other.
2. 1,354 is greater than 1,345 because it has 5 tens instead of 4 tens.
3. Answers will vary.

Page 26

1. 7,063
2. 3,492
3. 9,520
4. 7,677
5. 9,116
6. 5,091

Page 27

1. 5,552
2. 9,745
3. 7,535
4. 8,870
5. 4,423
6. 8,700

Page 28

1. Answers will vary.
2. 1,971; Explanations will vary.
3. Answers will vary.

Page 30

1. 4,061
2. 7,501
3. 3,352
4. 918
5. 1,094
6. 5,162

Page 31

1. 2,218
2. 4,453
3. 4,822
4. 1,098
5. 531
6. 3,509

Page 32

1. Answers will vary.
2. 2,638; Explanations may vary.
3. Answers will vary.

Answer Key *(cont.)*

Page 34

1. 1,712 (1,600 + 100 + 12)
2. 6,100 (4,000 + 2,000 + 80 + 20)
3. 13,440 (10,00 + 3,000 + 400 + 40)

Page 35

1. 11,342 (10,000 + 1,200 + 140 + 2)
2. 5,880 (5,400 + 480)
3. 12,603 (12,000 + 600 + 3)

Page 36

1. An area model helps me break down the multi-digit number into smaller multiplication problems. It also helps me see what I'm actually multiplying.
2. 9,120; I know this because 1,000 × 5 = 5,000; 800 × 5 = 4,000; 20 × 5 = 100; and 4 × 5 = 20. 5,000 + 4,000 + 100 + 20 = 9,120.
3. Answers will vary.

Page 38

1. 468	2. 444	3. 837	4. 915

Page 39

1. 672	2. 2,173	3. 1,102	4. 806

Page 40

1. An area model helps me break down the multi-digit numbers into expanded form to work with smaller multiplication problems that are easier to multiply.
2. 425; I know this because I multiplied 20 × 10 = 200, 20 × 7 = 140, 10 × 5 = 50, and 7 × 5 = 35. 200 + 140 + 50 + 35 = 425.
3. Answers will vary.

Page 42

1. 42	2. 36	3. 58

Page 43

1. 72	2. 17	3. 43

Page 44

1. Partial quotients are the smaller parts to the answer of a division problem. They help you divide because you can break down the problem into smaller pieces and find the quotients of those pieces. Then you add the partial quotients to find the final quotient to the problem.
2. You can use multiplication to check the answers to division problems.
3. Answers will vary.

Page 46

1. $\frac{1}{3}$	2. $\frac{6}{8}$	3. $\frac{6}{9}$	4. $\frac{10}{12}$

Page 47

1. $\frac{2}{4}$	3. $\frac{2}{3}$	5. $\frac{6}{8}$	7. $\frac{2}{4}$
2. $\frac{6}{12}$	4. $\frac{1}{4}$	6. $\frac{8}{12}$	8. $\frac{6}{10}$

Page 48

1. Two fractions are equivalent if they take up the same amount of space within the whole shape.
2. Yes, the pictures do represent equivalent fractions because the shaded portion of each shape takes up the same amount of space. $\frac{1}{3} = \frac{2}{6}$
3. Answers will vary.

Page 50

1. $>$	2. $<$	3. $<$	4. $>$	5. $>$	6. $<$

Page 51

1. $>$	3. $=$	5. $>$	7. $<$
2. $<$	4. $<$	6. $=$	8. $<$

Page 52

1. Comparing fractions means determining whether a fraction is greater than, less than, or equal to another fraction.
2. Yes, the inequality is true; Explanations may vary.
3. Answers will vary.

Page 54

1. $9\frac{2}{4}$ or $9\frac{1}{2}$	3. 12	5. $6\frac{3}{6}$ or $6\frac{1}{2}$
2. $4\frac{2}{3}$	4. 7	6. $9\frac{3}{8}$

Page 55

1. $11\frac{4}{8}$ or $11\frac{1}{2}$	3. $22\frac{2}{4}$ or $22\frac{1}{2}$	5. $13\frac{3}{5}$
2. $7\frac{5}{6}$	4. 11	6. $7\frac{4}{8}$ or $7\frac{1}{2}$

Page 56

1. A mixed number contains a whole number and a fraction.
2. $7\frac{4}{5}$; Explanations may vary.
3. Answers will vary.

Page 58

1. $3\frac{1}{3}$	3. $4\frac{6}{8}$ or $4\frac{3}{4}$	5. $3\frac{2}{9}$
2. $9\frac{2}{4}$ or $9\frac{1}{2}$	4. 2	6. $1\frac{3}{8}$

Page 59

1. $2\frac{6}{8}$ or $2\frac{3}{4}$	3. 6	5. $7\frac{1}{5}$
2. $3\frac{1}{4}$	4. $2\frac{1}{10}$	6. $\frac{1}{6}$

Page 60

1. Answers will vary but should include a whole number and a fraction.
2. Answers will vary but should include breaking the mixed number into smaller parts.
3. Answers will vary.

Page 62

1. $2\frac{1}{2}$ 2. $\frac{2}{8}$ or $\frac{1}{4}$ 3. 2 4. $\frac{9}{4}$ or $2\frac{1}{4}$

Page 63

1. $2\frac{2}{3}$
2. $2\frac{2}{4}$ or $2\frac{1}{2}$
3. $3\frac{3}{5}$
4. $\frac{3}{8}$

Page 64

1. Answers will vary but may include that they help show which parts show whole numbers and which parts show fractions.
2. An improper fraction has a numerator that is bigger than the denominator. It can be rewritten as a mixed number.
3. Answers will vary.

Page 66

1. 0.5
2. 0.72
3. 0.17
4. 0.3
5. 0.89
6. 0.9
7. 0.4
8. 0.40

Page 67

1. 0.2
2. 0.27
3. 0.34
4. 0.1
5. 0.05
6. 0.8
7. 0.6
8. 0.61

Page 68

1. You need to understand place value because decimal notation represents fractions that are less than one. These numbers use place value to the right of the decimal point.
2. Fractions and decimals are related because they both represent numbers that are less than one whole.
3. Answers will vary.

Page 70

1. $\frac{25}{100}$; $\frac{70}{100}$; $<$
2. $\frac{6}{10}$; $\frac{5}{10}$; $>$
3. $\frac{65}{100}$; $\frac{31}{100}$; $>$
4. $\frac{41}{100}$; $\frac{40}{100}$; $>$
5. $<$
6. $>$

Page 71

1. $\frac{43}{100}$; $\frac{40}{100}$; $>$
2. $\frac{30}{100}$; $\frac{35}{100}$; $<$
3. $\frac{8}{100}$; $\frac{80}{100}$; $<$
4. $\frac{75}{100}$; $\frac{70}{100}$; $>$
5. $>$
6. $<$

Page 72

1. Answers will vary.
2. Yes, the inequality is true. If you convert $\frac{3}{10}$ to hundredths, you get $\frac{30}{100}$, and that is less than $\frac{35}{100}$.
3. Answers will vary.

Page 74

1. 10 m
2. 5 km
3. 1,200 cm
4. 5 m
5. 4,000 m
6. 10 km

Page 75

1. 1 km
2. 50 m
3. 1,600 cm
4. 10,000 m
5. 7,000 m
6. 5 m

Page 76

1. You need to multiply or divide to convert measurements. For example, to find how many centimeters are in 5 meters, you need to multiply 5 times 100 because there are 100 centimeters for every 1 meter.
2. 9,000 meters; I know this because 1 km equals 1,000 meters. So, I multiplied 9 × 1,000 to get 9,000.
3. Answers will vary.

Page 78

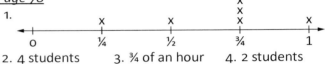

1. (number line)
   - 0
   - $\frac{1}{4}$: X
   - $\frac{1}{2}$: X
   - $\frac{3}{4}$: X X X
   - 1: X
2. 4 students
3. $\frac{3}{4}$ of an hour
4. 2 students

Page 79

1. 15 students
2. 6 students
3. 4 students
4. 4 students

Page 80

1. A line plot organizes data on a number line.
2. Answers will vary.
3. Answers will vary.

Page 82

1. line
2. ray
3. line segment
4. line
5. Pictures will vary but should show a four-sided closed figure.

Page 83

1.
2.
3.

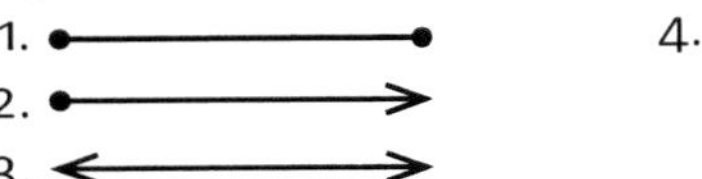

4. Pictures will vary but should show a three-sided closed figure.

Page 84

1. A ray continues forever in one direction but has an endpoint on the other side. A line goes continues forever in both directions.
2. A line segment is part of a line. It is has two endpoints, but a line does not have any endpoints.
3. Answers will vary.

Page 86

1. right 2. obtuse 3. acute 4. acute
5.

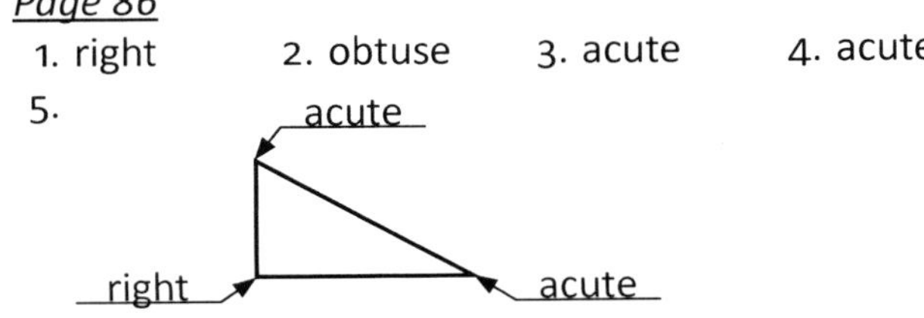

Page 87

1\.

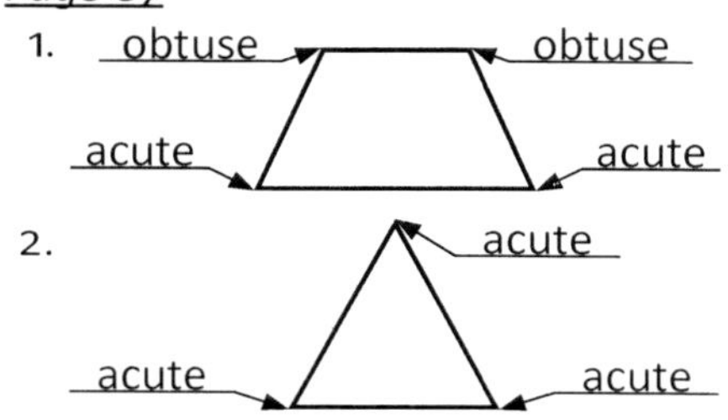

2\.

3. Drawings and labels will vary.

Page 88

1. The angle is obtuse. I know this because it is greater than 90 degrees.
2. Some figures have only one type of angle while others have each type of angle; Examples will vary.
3. Answers will vary.

Page 90

1. perpendicular
2. parallel
3. perpendicular
4. parallel
5. right
6. acute

Page 91

Drawings will vary but students should draw at least two figures for each category.

Page 92

1. Parallel lines are lines that will never intersect while perpendicular lines are lines that intersect to form a right angle.
2. Yes, a figure can be classified into more than one category. For example, the figure might have both parallel and perpendicular lines, such as a square or rectangle. A figure can also have different types of angles, so it might be classified as both acute and obtuse.
3. Answers will vary.

Page 94

1. yes
2. no
3. no
4. yes

5\.

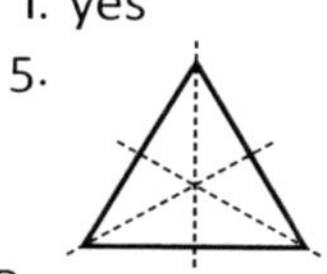

6\.

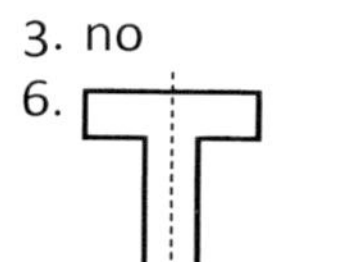

Page 95

1\. 3.

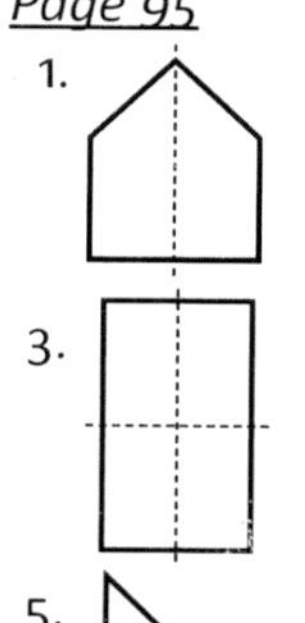

2\. 4.

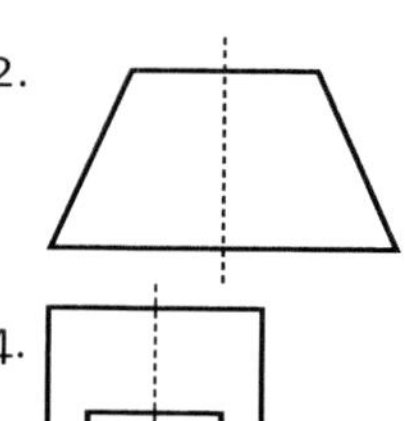

5\.

6\.

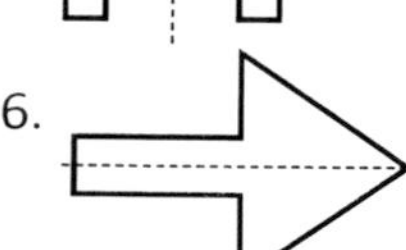

Page 96

1. A line of symmetry is an imaginary line that divides a figure into two equal halves.
2. The figure does not have a line of symmetry because there is no way to divide it in half and have identical, equal parts.
3. Answers will vary.

Page 98

1. Sona will read 288 pages.
2. Mr. Lee can feed 40 students.

Page 99

1. There will be 46 students on each bus.
2. Each friend will get 13 stickers.

Page 100

1. A multistep word problem is a problem that requires more than one step in order to find the answer. These problems often use two or more operations.
2. Answers will vary.

Page 102

1. I run $2\frac{1}{3}$ miles in a week.
2. I spent $3\frac{3}{4}$ hours reading after 5 days.

Page 103

1. There is $\frac{4}{10}$ (or $\frac{2}{5}$) of a pizza left.
2. Four people will drink $2\frac{2}{5}$ liters of punch.

Page 104

1. Visual models help you see the problem to help you solve it.
2. The answer falls between 2 and 3 on the number line. I know this because the fraction in all is $2\frac{2}{3}$, which is greater than 2 but less than 3.

Page 106

1. 160 ounces
2. 107 lbs.
3. $8.95
4. 5 meters

Page 107

1. 28 miles
2. 80 ounces
3. 5,000 meters
4. Yes; 27¢ left over

Page 108

1. Answers will vary.
2. Answers will vary.